ANOTHER CHANCE

How GOD Overrides OUR BIG MISTAKES

DEAN MERRILL

ZONDERVAN PUBLISHING HOUSE
OF THE ZONDERVAN CORPORATION
GRAND RAPIDS, MICHIGAN 49506

Unless otherwise indicated, the *New International Version of the Holy Bible* (© 1978 by New York International Bible Society) has been used. Additional translations are *King James Version* (KJV), *Living Bible* (LB), and *Revised Standard Version* (RSV).

Names and other identifications in the profiles of Part Four have been changed at the request of the subjects.

Pages 59–64 reprinted from *Where Eagles Soar* © 1980 by Jamie Buckingham. Published by Chosen Books Publishing Co., Ltd., Lincoln, VA 22078. Used by permission.

Pages 117–120 excerpted from *Let Us Enjoy Forgiveness* by Judson Cornwall © 1978 by Judson Cornwall. Published by Fleming H. Revell Company. Used by permission.

Pages 123–124 reprinted with permission from "Waiting" © 1978 by Christian Medical Society.

ANOTHER CHANCE: How God Overrides Our Big Mistakes
© 1981 by The Zondervan Corporation
Grand Rapids, Michigan

Second printing January 1982

Library of Congress Cataloging in Publication Data

Merrill, Dean.
    Another chance.

    Includes bibliographical references.
    1. Christian life—1960– . 2. Providence and government of God. I. Title.
BV4501.2.M45   248.4   81-16483
ISBN 0-310-35331-9   AACR2

Designed by Martha Bentley
Edited by Louise H. Rock

Printed in the United States of America

Contents

Restoration

The sheep goes now
Toward the distant slope
Where taller, tastier grass awaits.
Let the ninety and nine stay bleating and bumping one another—
The horizon calls.

He's one of your flock, Good Shepherd,
And he's heading for the ravine.
He doesn't understand drop-offs
And wolves
And how soon darkness will fall upon the land.
Call him back! Stop him!

The meadow shrinks in the gathering dusk
And the Shepherd's ram,
Full but unsatisfied,
Edges toward the rim
Until in a clatter of gravel and dust
He plummets into the gorge
Brambles clawing at his wool—
He lies stunned upon his back.

He cannot rise; he cannot reverse
The steps that brought him to this dreadful place;
He can, in fact, do nothing at all.
A cold moon stares down at him
While sounds of night intensify;
He is trapped—but more
He is alone.

A flickering lamp, footsteps in the underbrush,
The chill and darkness are foiled this time
As muscled arms encircle the fallen one
And hoist him from the stones and mud
To ride upon tall shoulders
Back to the village fold.

Had you nothing else to do this night, Good Shepherd?
Should not this rebel sheep of yours be ousted
From care and food and drink for this?
He chose his independent path—
Will he yet be welcome in your flock?

He answers not; he is too busy
Calling friends and neighbors,
The young and old about the town,
And even angels hear his shout:
"Rejoice with me! I have found
My sheep which was lost!
He was mine before; he is mine tonight;
He shall be mine forever!
Rejoice, rejoice."

The villagers cheer,
And light years distant,
The cherubim slap each other
On the back—
Both earth and heaven are awake tonight
For the jubilee that crowns
The restoration of a single sheep.

PART ONE

The Return of Confidence

The God of
the Second Chance

I believe in the God of the second chance.

I believe in the God who is not put off by our fiascos.

I believe in the God who has an uncanny ability to bring good out of disaster.

I believe in the God who puts Humpty Dumpties back together again.

He is the God, in fact, whose "mercy endureth forever." How many times have we recited those words without absorbing their meaning. His mercy has no cutoff. It goes on . . . and on . . . and on. . . .

It endures for the person who has made an undeniable mistake in his life, whose future has been torpedoed by one or more fateful acts. The person who has stepped outside of his marriage . . . the trusted employee who has mishandled corporate funds . . . the woman who has borne an illegitimate child . . . the young man who has rejected his early faith and turned instead to drugs or alcohol . . . the person who has betrayed his family, his friends. . . .

Divine mercy reaches as well to the person who has not

committed an overt act of wrong, but has rather made a bad decision. It made sense enough at the time of choosing, but with hindsight, it turns out to have been tragic. The person who left a job when he should have stayed . . . or stayed when he should have left . . . or married the wrong person in a moment of haste . . . or quit school too soon, thereby limiting future advancement . . . or got into hopeless debt . . . or sent his child to the wrong school, triggering a barrage of negative effects . . . or started a business that flopped.

Does God hold on to such children? When their dreams have been smashed, when self-confidence has fled, when the future goes blank, when even fellow Christians shake their heads and look the other way—is the Father's patience exhausted, too?

Let him speak for himself:

> "I will restore you to health
> and heal your wounds,"
> declares the LORD,
> "because you are called an outcast,
> Zion for whom no one cares."
> *Jeremiah* 30:17

> I live in a high and holy place,
> but also with him who is contrite and lowly in spirit,
> to revive the spirit of the lowly
> and to revive the heart of the contrite.
> I will not accuse forever,
> nor will I always be angry,
> for then the spirit of man would grow faint before me—
> the breath of man that I have created.
> I have seen his ways, but I will heal him;
> I will guide him and restore comfort to him.
> *Isaiah* 57:15–16, 18

David, who made more than one spectacular error and was still hailed in the New Testament as a man who "served God's purpose in his own generation" (Acts 13:36), gives us some touching glimpses of the God he knew:

I will exalt you, O LORD,
   for you lifted me out of the depths.
You turned my wailing into dancing;
   you removed my sackcloth and clothed me with joy,
that my heart may sing to you and not be silent.
   O LORD my God, I will give you thanks forever.
   Psalm 30:1, 11–12

It is at this point—"Who is God, and what kind of God is he?"—that we must begin. We must return to our Source, our Refuge. What he thinks of us, now that we have blown it, will have a greater impact on our future than almost anything else.

We may fear to approach him; in fact, he may be the *last* person we want to confront, schooled as we are in teachings about his blazing holiness, his disgust for sin, his absolute purity.

But on the other hand, he has been watching over a planet of imperfect children for a very long time. What we have done was hardly a shock to him. He has seen it many times before. Furthermore, he is the only one who has both the power and the will to redeem the situation.

The advice of our times can mislead us. We are told, in various ways, "To move back to former things is regression. Faith is an element of childhood. Belief is something you cling to in your early crises, until you come to a more mature way of coping."

The good news to adults who have made a major mistake in their lives is this: *It's okay to run to your Father.* In fact, it's the smartest thing you can do at the moment. It is your one route to freedom from the confusion, guilt, shame, and self-doubt that hammer at your sanity. In the words of Paul Johnson's contemporary Christian song:

> He didn't bring us this far to leave us;
> He didn't teach us to swim to let us drown.
> He didn't build his home in us to move away;
> He didn't lift us up to let us down.

In the ancient world, a well-known legend told about a

17

rather marvelous bird called the phoenix, which lived in splendor in the Far East. Its home was a grove of trees untouched by violence, fear, or grief of any kind, perpetually green and verdant. The phoenix passed its time with singing and reveling in utopian joys on all sides.

But once every five hundred years, she left her home for the world of death. She flew to Syria, built a nest in the top of a palm tree, and set fire to herself. Amazingly, from her ashes a worm emerged, which developed a cocoon and soon became a new, young phoenix bird ready to return to the East and begin the life-cycle again.

A farfetched myth—except that more than a few early Christians saw within it an illustration of a central theme of the Gospel: resurrection. Clement of Rome retold the story in his *First Letter* (chapters 25–26) as he was making the point that God brings life out of death, not only in the case of his Son, but in us as well. We are the receivers of something inextinguishable: eternal life, a force meant to show itself in the present as well as the future. In the midst of a world that is dying, we can rise from our own ashes. We can live again.

Says Paul: "We have this treasure in jars of clay to show that this all-surpassing power is from God and not from us. We are hard pressed on every side, but not crushed; perplexed, but not in despair; persecuted, but not abandoned; struck down, but not destroyed. We always carry around in our body the death of Jesus, so that the life of Jesus may also be revealed in our body. For we who are alive are always being given over to death for Jesus' sake, so that his life may be revealed in our mortal body.

"Therefore we do not lose heart. Though outwardly we are wasting away, yet inwardly we are being renewed day by day. So *we fix our eyes* not on what is seen, but *on what is unseen.* For what is seen is temporary, but what is unseen is eternal" (2 Cor. 4:7–11, 16, 18, italics added).

The eternal God is not about to be stymied. The present chaos is not the end of things. His life in us will triumph.

* * *

And that is what the rest of this book is about. It will show you some of the means God uses to bring life out of death, renewed potential out of disappointment and downfall. It will introduce you to people who have been through a self-inflicted ordeal and have come through to sunshine once again. They are not perfect people; they have not necessarily done everything right since their fall. They are rather a cross-section to show that restoration *can* happen. Their stories and the other parts of this book will help you answer the question "Where do I go from here?"

The Holy Spirit, after all, is called the Counselor four different times in Scripture. Long before modern psychotherapy began trying to help persons in stress, the Spirit was restoring and renewing, guiding men and women through the white water rapids of their lives to the quiet pools beyond. He is the same today.

For Your Reflection

1. What was your view of God as a child? Was he most like a judge? A grandfather? A school principal? What?

2. Now that you're older, how do you view him? Has he become friendlier over the years? More stern? Or about the same?

3. What did you read in this chapter that made you say, "Yes, but—"? Were your objections valid?

4. If you really believed that God gave second chances in this life, what differences would it make in your feelings about yourself?

What Now?

*If I found I had driven into a bog, I should know I had
missed the road. But this knowledge would not be of
much comfort if I then had to stand helpless watching the
car sink and vanish: the damage would be done, and that
would be that. Is it the same when a Christian wakes up
to the fact that he has missed God's guidance and taken
the wrong way? Is the damage irrevocable? Must he now
be put off course for life? Thank God, no. Our God is a
God who not merely restores, but takes up our mistakes
and follies into His plan for us and brings good out of
them. This is part of the wonder of His gracious
sovereignty. 'I will restore to you the years that the lo-
cust has eaten. . . .' God makes not only the wrath of
man to turn to His praise but the misadventures of
Christians too.*

— J. I. Packer
Knowing God, *pp. 219–20*

A Little Thing
Called Hope

He began with all the right connections. His mother was a prominent woman in the Jerusalem church, their spacious home a meeting place for part of the huge congregation. The apostle Peter had come to their door first upon his miraculous release from prison (Acts 12) to break the news that prayer had been answered.

His cousin was the gentle, respected Barnabas, donor of real-estate funds to the work of the church, "a good man, full of the Holy Spirit and faith" (Acts 11:24). Thus it was not a total surprise that when Barnabas and Paul were set apart by the Antioch believers for the first missionary journey, a historic new venture into the Mediterranean world, "John was with them as their helper" (Acts 13:5). His future was bright.

But sometime in the next few weeks, all that changed. The Scriptures do not tell us why or how. Perhaps the crossing of the open water to Cyprus was frightening; perhaps the tension of the appearance before the proconsul, when Paul suddenly called for a sorcerer to be struck blind, took its toll. Perhaps the young man was irritated at the secondary role that was falling to his relative as Paul's ministry flourished. Whatever the cause,

John Mark stuck it out for one more voyage, to Perga on the mainland, and then made the mistake of his life. He "left them to return to Jerusalem" (Acts 13:13).

What he said upon his arrival we do not know. But we do know that he had seared his worthlessness into the memory of Paul. Two years later, when Paul and Barnabas began planning their second extended trip abroad, the name of John Mark was raised. "Absolutely not," declared the apostle. "He deserted us last time. He's useless."

Barnabas could not agree, and invited his cousin to go along on a separate mission to Cyprus. But we cannot help noticing in Acts 15:40 that it was Paul and his new associate, Silas, who left "commended by the brothers to the grace of the Lord." Their exploits take up the next two and one-half chapters of the Bible, while not a further word is said about Barnabas and John Mark's trip.

Was his career forever doomed? Could God do anything with a quitter? Would the church ever give him another opportunity?

Fifteen years pass before the answer comes, in the writings of Paul from a Roman prison. His traveling days are now finished; he must rely upon his pen and his colleagues in the ministry:

"My fellow prisoner Aristarchus sends you his greetings, as does Mark, the cousin of Barnabas. (You have received instructions about him; if he comes to you, welcome him)" (Col. 4:10).

"Epaphras . . . sends you greetings. And so do Mark, Aristarchus, Demas and Luke, my fellow workers" (Philem. 23–24).

And in Paul's final note to Timothy, perhaps just weeks before his execution, he has this request:

"Get Mark and bring him with you, because he is helpful to me in my ministry" (2 Tim. 4:11).

But the greatest evidence of John Mark's restoration is still to come. It is he—the undependable one—who records the second of the four gospels, an exciting, action-packed account of the life of our Lord. His place in history is thus assured forever.

* * *

If there is hope for John Mark, there is hope for us today. Few of us have squandered as much potential as he. His story, tucked into corners of the New Testament, is an inspiring example of starting again.

And it is inspiration, the glimmer of hope, of expectation, that we desperately need in the aftermath of our own stumblings. The Bible has more to say about hope than we have realized. We have been caught up with more impressive things. "And now abideth faith, hope, love, these three; but the greatest of these is love" (see 1 Cor. 13:13).

If love is the greatest . . . which is the least?

It is hope.

Hope is not strong enough to reach out to others, as love does. Hope can never move mountains—that requires genuine faith. Hence, we brush hope aside as minor, auxiliary, an extra. We don't hear many sermons about it. We don't write songs in its honor.

What is hope, anyway?

It is a quiet voice that says, "Maybe . . ." It softly reminds us that there is a faint possibility of a comeback.

Hope is actually very close to fear. Fear looks at a set of grim prospects and says, "It might fail." Hope looks at the same set of grim prospects . . . and says, "It might work."

Hope and fear are thus like two ships passing in the night, but headed in opposite directions. They are at the same dark, murky point in the ocean. But by morning, they will be miles apart.

Because hope keeps saying, "Well, *it's possible.*" Hope just may blossom someday into something impressive like faith. That is why Hebrews 11:1 defines faith as "being sure of what we hope for." In the beginning we are not sure at all. We know too well that it is ridiculous to put hope in ourselves. We have already demonstrated our own shortcomings. We can only hope that God is wise enough to make something beautiful out of our messed-up lives. We can only recognize that *it's possible*. At some future point we may be sure that he can and will, and that's faith. But for now . . .

I sat talking with a man in his fifties who had broken the chains of alcoholism nineteen years before and has worked with other alcoholics ever since. "Where do you begin?" I asked.

"The first step is to restore confidence," he answered readily. "Everything else must wait until the problem drinker is led to see that he or she just might make it this time. I tell them my story; I give them God's promises; I introduce them to other ex-alcoholics who have conquered—all to make that first crucial point. Once there's hope, we're on our way."

Jonathan, son of King Saul in the Old Testament, shows us what can happen to a hopeful attitude. In 1 Samuel 14, he and his father's army are in a desperate situation. The Philistines have five times as many chariots as Saul has *men;* his troops have dwindled to a mere six hundred. Saul can't make up his mind what to do; his options are severely restricted. The Philistines have long ago seized all the Israelite blacksmiths, leaving the army with almost no usable weaponry. The cold fact is that they are now simply waiting to die.

Does Jonathan stand and rally his father's men with an impassioned speech full of faith?

No. He can only muster a scrap of hope. He turns to one other person, his young armor-bearer, and suggests going over to the Philistine outpost. Why?

"Perhaps the LORD will act in our behalf. Nothing can hinder the LORD from saving, whether by many or by few" (1 Sam. 14:6).

Notice, he's making no predictions. He's simply stating a fact: *it's possible.*

The two young men gingerly let themselves be seen by the swaggering Philistines. "Come up to us and we'll teach you a lesson," the guards shout. Before the day is over, it is the other way around; the Israelites have won a stunning victory.

That's what hope can do, given a chance to grow. People in

trouble often say, "I don't want to get my hopes up." Yes! Get them up! The Scripture promises in Romans 5:5 that "hope does not disappoint us, because God has poured out his love into our hearts by the Holy Spirit, whom he has given us." We have good reason to hope. If God is the kind of God he said he was in the previous section of this book, then we are quite justified in being hopeful. Romans 8:22–24 even goes so far as to describe God's intention to redeem us from this world of groaning and pain and then says: "For in this hope we were saved." Salvation is ours on so slender a platform as hope? Yes. Because hope is another word for confidence, and confidence in the Savior's work is all that is required.

A speaker named Doug Wead (whose sermon inspired much of this chapter) teases his audiences occasionally by asking, "Do you know what my favorite verse in all of Scripture is? It's none of the great classics—John 3:16, the Twenty-third Psalm, etc. My favorite, believe it or not, is Ecclesiastes 9:4." And then he quotes:

"Anyone who is among the living has hope—even a live dog is better off than a dead lion!"

He always draws a laugh, but his point is serious. More of us identify with dogs than with lions. We don't expect to be kings of the modern jungle. Yet even dogs can have hope.

Jesus spent most of his ministry reaching out to people who were sick, mistaken, unsure, a disappointment to themselves, tired. He did so, Matthew explains, to fulfill Isaiah's prophecy:

> A bruised reed he will not break,
>> and a smoldering wick he will not snuff out,
> till he leads justice to victory.
>> In his name the nations will put their hope.
>> *Matthew* 12:20–21

Can we recover our balance after we have fallen? Can the pieces be put together again? Can we smile again, laugh again, love again? Can we, like John Mark, ever regain a place of usefulness?

It's possible.

For Your Reflection

1. People sometimes belittle hope as not being productive; they consider it a waste of time. How would you answer that?

2. Which hopes of yours have been shattered in the past? Were they hopes based on human beings, or hopes based on what God might do?

3. Spend some time meditating on Lamentations 3:19–33. What does this passage mean to you personally?

PROFILE

The "Creative Borrower"

What makes a bright young woman—an honor student throughout school, and raised in the church—decide to defraud the bank she works for? And after she's caught and sent to federal prison, how does she go on living when she gets out?

Jackie Scott grew up on a farm outside a small South Carolina town, the third of four daughters. She was an early achiever; she brought home straight-A report cards; she became a cheerleader and a basketball player in high school; she even won a local beauty contest. Her father, who had two businesses in town besides his farming, drank too much, but her mother was a devout Christian, and Jackie joined the Southern Baptist church at the age of 12. "I guess I was a 'good girl,'" she says, "—didn't dance, swear, or drink. In my community, church was the thing to do, and we were all very active."

Her adolescent faith got its first test, however, two weeks after graduation, when the family home burned to the ground. Before the summer was over, an older sister's little boy had died after ingesting a household chemical. "I blamed God for this sudden avalanche of trouble," Jackie recalls in her soft Carolina accent, "and when I left for Winthrop College that September" (a women's college in Rock Hill, South Carolina, that had awarded her a scholarship), "I didn't work too hard at finding a church to attend." More of her time was spent in partying, since her studies continued to come easily.

The petite, brown-haired coed went home the next summer to an eerie replay of the year before. Incredibly, the new house that had been built on the farm caught fire and was destroyed. Her father entered yet another alcoholism treatment program, this one involving electroshock therapy.

When he returned in August, much of his memory was gone. He didn't even recognize Jackie, and a few days later, he ended his life with a gun.

"Questions began pounding in my mind. *If I'd been a better daughter, would he have taken his life? Could I have tried harder somehow?* I had few answers, of course. In an effort to cope, I soon began turning off my emotions, walling myself in from all joy or pain."

Back at school, she met a man, recently graduated, who was able to unlock the tightness within her. His happy, carefree manner attracted her, and six months later she dropped out of college to become Mrs. Jackie Butner. She'd been majoring in mathematics and business, so it was only natural that she should be hired as an administrative assistant at a bank in Columbia, the state capital.

Her job went better than her marriage; she soon discovered that her husband could not control his drinking. A sense of *deja vu* swept over her as she realized how similar her situation was to her mother's—only this husband was not interested in seeking help. "So I threw my energy into my work," she says. "The bank was facing a possible loss of $1.5

million on student loans. They gave me the project of chasing down the students and trying to collect. I managed to cut the potential loss to $150,000."

But then the program was turned over to a male officer, while Jackie was made an assistant branch manager. Her boss gave her wide responsibility for the twelve tellers and two secretaries who worked there, and also for training the new men just out of college. "I began noticing a pattern: the guys I would train would inevitably be promoted to branch manager somewhere else. Branch managers were officers of the bank, while we assistant managers were not, and there was a good $5,000 difference between the two. It happened time and again.

"I felt taken advantage of, and I began thinking about how to get what I believed was mine." The day came when Jackie decided to type up papers for a sixty-day loan to a nonexisting person. The proceeds of the loan were deposited in a checking account, from which she then began to draw money to invest in real estate around town. "It was so easy," she remembers. "I could run credits and debits through the system almost at will, and there was no matching up to see what went where. The bank's internal auditors missed it, and so did the federal auditors."

When the loan had to be repaid after two months, Jackie simply processed a new loan to cover the first. As time went by, her property values appreciated, and she kept her bogus accounts in good order. "Over a two-year period, I probably cleared only about three or four thousand dollars in profit, so this wasn't a big scam. But I was enjoying my quiet revenge against the sexism of the institution.

"Once in a great while, when I'd sit down to make out a new set of papers, I'd say, 'God, if you'll let me get away with this once more, I'll quit.' It was little more than words, and he knew it as well as I did."

The seeds of trouble were sown when Jackie finally did receive a promotion to assistant operations manager of the branch bank in her hometown. "That meant I had to move my loans so I could keep an eye on them. I lumped all of my indebtedness together into one loan at the branch where I was going, and this time I used my mother's name. I figured I was safe, since she had no accounts at my bank."

Jackie's growing fund was now invested in a classic old Southern plantation-style home that needed restoration. She plunged into the project during her off-hours, bringing the mansion to its former grandeur. She was so busy, in fact, that one month it finally happened—she forgot to make a payment. The bank's computer promptly generated a delinquent notice, which was mailed to Jackie's mother.

"I was over at mom's one day, and she said, 'Jackie, what's this thing I got from your bank? I don't have any mortgage at your bank.'

"I fought back the panic as I snatched the envelope from her hand. 'Oh, who knows?' I responded. 'Somebody must have goofed up . . . never mind, I'll handle it.'" But when Jackie left that day, she forgot and left the notice lying on the counter.

Her conscientious mother then sat down to write to the bank and advise that an error had apparently been made, that she had no account with them. A few days later, a collection officer called.

"Mrs. Scott, your letter is a bit strange, since I have here in front of me the loan application in your name. And furthermore, you've been making your payments right on time for many months now."

"Why, I can't imagine—!"

"The loan is all properly executed and authorized by an officer of our bank, Jackie Butner."

A gasp, and then, "Well, that's my daughter—but I still . . ."

The collections officer hung up and immediately called for an auditor. They pulled all of the loans Jackie had ever approved and sent out audit notices, the kind that say, "If these figures are correct, please discard; if not, let us know."

At least a dozen came back stamped "No such person at this address."

*   *   *

The date was December 31, 1974, and Jackie Butner was hurrying to wrap up a number of loose ends before the close of the fiscal year. She instructed her secretary not to disturb her as she set about her work. With any luck she could finish early and get home to prepare for a New Year's Eve party she and her husband were throwing that evening.

About 10:30 A.M., there was a knock at her door. The secretary timidly announced that the bank president was on the phone.

With a touch of irritation, Jackie stopped what she was doing and picked up the receiver to hear, "Jackie, come to Columbia. Your branch manager will drive you."

In a flash Jackie saw that delinquent notice still lying on her mother's ledge. She grabbed her loan file from her desk drawer, ran outside to lock it in her car trunk, and then joined her boss for the silent sixty-mile ride to the head office. As she watched the fields and trees rush past her window, she kept bracing herself. *Stay cool, Jackie. You can handle it. You might lose your job, but that's all. Don't let them intimidate you.*

In the meeting, the auditors presented what they had uncovered so far. It was established that a total of $19,960 was outstanding. Jackie remained calm, making mental notes of what the investigators still didn't know. Finally she said,

"What do you want from me?"

The president cleared his throat. "Your resignation."

Jackie nodded her head and proceeded to write it out on the spot. She handed it to the head auditor and then made a suggestion to meet again in the new year to review the details and straighten out the records.

"Wait a minute, Jackie—someone else wants to talk to you."

"Who?"

"The FBI."

The men in the white shirts and black ties were ushered into the room, and Jackie suddenly began to feel sick inside. Things were going further than she had planned. A federal investigation would be opened, they said, and she would come to the next meeting with her attorney. . . .

As soon as the meeting broke up, she dashed to a telephone to call her husband. "Come pick me up in Columbia," she urged, not taking time to explain why. As soon as he arrived, the two of them sped to a branch of the bank, where she cleaned out her personal savings and checking accounts before any stop orders could be placed on them.

"Then I told him of the accusations, and what had been going on over the last two years. He had known nothing up to then; in fact, we'd been growing further and further apart in almost all areas. Neither of us were working at the relationship any more. Naturally, he was now very hurt and angry at what I had done."

Within two days, he left. The long-untended marriage was over, and a divorce followed in time.

Jackie's attorney, upon reviewing the evidence of her financial cunning, had two quick words of advice: 1. Cooperate with the bank all you can—there's no way to get out of this. 2. Find a therapist, because the trauma of what's ahead for you is going to be very tough.

When Jackie met again with the president, she came with a penitent attitude. All the facts were laid out in the open, and she promised to repay all the money as soon as she could sell the plantation house; the bank would lose nothing in the end.

The man leaned back in his executive chair and began talking about his own daughter, who had recently been charged with smoking pot. "You know, Jackie," he mused, "you're a lot like her. You don't need to be prosecuted; what you need is to be put over my knee and given a good spanking. But now that the FBI is in on it . . . well, we'll do what we can to make things easiest for you."

The days to come, however, were anything but easier for the accused embezzler whose husband had just left her. In mid-January, Jackie began to realize that on top of everything else, she was pregnant. "It was just about more than I could handle, and even my psychiatrist was of limited help, because I couldn't afford to be honest with him. I kept holding back, maintaining my image, always remembering that at some point he would have to write a report about me for the judge."

Her case came before the grand jury in February—a total of twenty-one fraudulent transactions, each worth five years in jail. The thought of a 105-year sentence boggled her mind. But the bank's lawyers asked that the indictment be reduced to seven counts of embezzlement. The first hearing was set for March 21.

The first tiny hint that God was regulating the pressure in Jackie Butner's chaotic life came on March 20—in the form of a miscarriage. The next day's hearing was postponed as she lay in Baptist Hospital in Columbia recuperating from a D & C. Her first hours were spent in the maternity ward, until her therapist insisted that she be transferred. The only available space was in the psychiatric ward, where she spent an

35

exasperating weekend. Finally she just left her bed and walked out without permission.

"My body recovered all right, but not my spirits," Jackie remembers. "My doctor had me on lots of medication, and now I had to wait until May to go to court. I really couldn't see very many reasons for staying in this world. I had ruined just about everything I had valued.

"I was watching over a friend's apartment while she traveled in Europe, and the thought came to me one day that this would be a perfect place for a suicide. I went to the apartment that evening, gulped down a handful of Elavil tablets, and crawled into her bed to await the end. I pulled the covers up over my head and wondered what it would be like to die.

"The next thing I knew, I was in a hospital emergency room having my stomach pumped. I had neglected to turn off one light in the apartment, and a neighbor, who also had a key, had spotted it. She knew that no one should be in the apartment at that hour, so she came to check, and she found me.

"When I got out of the hospital this time, I returned to my apartment, and for the first time in years I began to pray. 'God,' I said, 'you must want me to be alive after all. The miscarriage, and now this—I guess you haven't forgotten about me.' This was my point of beginning again. I didn't tell anyone about that prayer, nor did I even go back to church except when my mother coaxed me into going with her. But a slow, gradual process had begun."

At the hearing in May, Jackie's attorney entered a plea of guilty to one count of embezzlement. He, of course, cited the fact that the money had now been repaid in full, that no loss had been sustained. The judge, however, delayed sentencing until a pscyhiatric study could be completed over a two-month period.

"I had hopes, naturally, that I could avoid prison,

but I didn't really expect that to happen. I figured it might be part of my payment." When the sentence was announced on August 1, a Friday, the judge noted that this was a first offense by a fairly young person. But it was a serious crime nevertheless, and for it Jackie would serve two years.

She held her breath, waiting for him to say something about a suspended sentence.

"You will report on August 15, two weeks from today, to the federal corrections facility at Lexington, Kentucky." His gavel came down, and that was all.

*   *   *

Few convicted felons ever went to jail more civilly. On that Friday morning, Jackie packed her red American Traveller suitcase, put on a trim-looking business suit that she had often worn to the bank, and boarded a flight to Lexington alone. Upon her arrival, she asked a woman in the airport washroom if there was any bus service out to the prison.

"Oh," said the woman, "my daughter's taking me out that way. We'll drop you by."

When they pulled up to the gate, Jackie collected her things and offered to pay the daughter. "Oh, no," she said cheerily. "Glad to help you. Have a nice visit!"

The guard at the gate took one look and assumed Jackie had come to apply for a job. Only gradually did the prison staff locate the paperwork and realize they had another inmate to sign in. But before nightfall, Jackie found herself in a noisy, crowded women's barrack with only a bed and a few square feet of aisle to call her own. That evening, for the first time in her life, she saw an all-out physical fight. One woman armed with a lead pipe wanted a different TV channel than another woman who wielded a razor blade inside a toothbrush.

That Sunday, August 17, was Jackie's

twenty-fourth birthday. A male inmate in the yard approached her with a smile and said, "Welcome—here's your present," as he handed her a joint of marijuana. But the day was most memorable for what happened as she sat in the prison chapel for the Protestant service.

"Something inside me seemed to say, *This will be your home. You'll find yourself here.* I don't remember which hymns we sang that morning, nor what the chaplain said. But I knew in my heart that I belonged here."

She was assigned a secretarial job in the prison's business office, and much of her free time in the weeks that followed was spent in the chapel. "It felt good just to sit at the piano and play the old songs," Jackie recalls wistfully. "Also, I got into a nightly Bible study of about eight to ten women. Gradually my faith began to come alive again.

"I was harassed and tested at the beginning, like any new inmate. But I was able to handle it, because Christ was helping me." She was eventually moved to an honor unit for good behavior, which allowed more freedom. Her room became an informal counseling center, where women would gather for long talks about spiritual things.

Fall passed into winter, and early in 1976, she was informed that she had been selected to go to Washington, D.C., for a two-week seminar being sponsored by Charles Colson, the former Nixon aide who was now trying to help prisoners. Jackie knew little about Colson, not having been politically minded, but the opportunity sounded exciting. "It was a tremendous experience for me, sitting in seminars all day with thirteen other prisoners, getting to meet people who knew where I was, putting a firmer foundation under my faith." She returned to Lexington with mounting enthusiasm.

As it turned out, her Washington friends provided more than good wishes when it came time for Jackie's parole board hearing the next month. To be eligible for parole, she would need a job and a place to live, and she had neither. Several possibilities had fallen through, and she prayed the night before, "Lord, if you want me to stay here a while longer, I'm willing to stay."

Only when she came before the board did she learn that the Colson group had arranged for a doctor in South Carolina to sponsor her upon release. On April 12, she walked out into the springtime to begin a three-month stay at a Methodist halfway house back in Columbia. The doctor took her to a laymen's breakfast the next morning—and who should sit across the table from her but the district attorney who had prosecuted her case! The man was a Christian, and when he asked Jackie what she hoped to do now, she softly replied, "I'd like to try to help those I left behind."

But for the time being, she worked as temporary secretary. Her first employer offered her a permanent job after just a few days, and was shocked to learn that Jackie had been in federal prison only last week! Eventually she ended up working for her former attorneys.

Her release date, when she would no longer be restricted to the halfway house, had been set for July 12, 1976. The last weeks, however, were anything but smooth. One night in late June she discovered something hard in one breast. A doctor referred her to a surgeon, who said that a biopsy would be necessary to see if it was cancerous. But that meant going into a hospital overnight—which was against the rules of her parole. Jackie groaned when she learned that the procedure would have to be done in the prison hospital back in Lexington.

"So I flew back, at government expense this time, to the one place on earth I never thought I'd have to see again as an inmate. It was a terrible night as I came marching across the commons, having to keep step with the guard at my side, while all my friends came running to the windows and doors gasping, 'What's Jackie doing back here?! Did she go PV (parole violator)? What's going on?' And I couldn't stop to answer them till I got to my place!

"I spent the Bicentennial weekend back in prison, waiting for surgery. Paul Kramer, one of Chuck Colson's assistants, called to let me know that all of them were praying for me, and others as well around the country. It was a long wait regardless. Finally, on Tuesday morning, July 5, I was prepared for surgery. The prison surgeon came in, reached down to make one last check . . .

". . . and the lump was gone.

"I was absolutely ecstatic. God had shown beyond any doubt that he still knew all about me and would intervene in my behalf."

A week later, Jackie was free on parole and headed for Washington, where she soon joined the Prison Fellowship staff as Charles Colson's secretary. "I found myself in my element—it was exactly what I wanted to do. Chuck's book *Born Again* had just been released then, and the calls for his time as a public speaker were flooding in. I was soon invited to speak to groups myself, and of course there were more and more groups of prisoners from all over the nation coming for two-week seminars, just as I had come."

Her job was not without its pressures, especially from promoters eager to exploit the Colson fame. At times Jackie bristled in the face of seeming hypocrisy, and once she admitted as much to a *Washingtonian* magazine reporter, who quoted her in print. She recalls, "I may have said more than I should have, but at least it got some things out into the open. After that I was able to quit playing games with the public. I was able to be myself, to describe our work with prisoners as it really was, and not worry about impressions."

In the spring of 1978, a friend invited her to attend a Sunday school class on "The Bible and ERA" being taught by a well-credentialed young scientist named David Bright. Jackie enjoyed the class and appreciated many of the ideas she heard. Her friend saw romantic possibilities in it all, but Jackie held back. "If the Lord wants anything like that to develop," she announced, "he will really have to bring it about."

He did. On September 16, 1978, Jackie and David were married. She left her position at Prison Fellowship in order to slow down the pace of her life and give full attention to her marriage. They settled in the Maryland suburb of Gaithersburg, and soon another surprise pregnancy came along, but this time it was a cause for gladness.

"I used to worry sometimes about bringing a child into the world," Jackie says now, "and how I'd explain about my past. Would it cause problems? Would other kids taunt my children about their mother having spent time in prison?

"But now that little Jennifer is here, it's not a problem. Someday I'll tell her, when she can understand it all. For now, God has given me a new life, a new future in which to honor him.

"I don't think of myself as an ex-con. I'm a Christian; I'm David's wife; I'm Jennifer's mother; I'm a volunteer who works on special projects for the Fellowship from time to time. I'm an example of 1 Corinthians 1:27, a verse that has meant much to me: 'But God chose the foolish things of the world to shame the wise; God chose the weak things of the world to shame the strong.' My foolishness is in the past now, and from here on, my life belongs to him."

PROFILE

The Cop Who Broke the Rules

If you were looking for seedbeds of adultery, you'd probably skip over the quiet river town of Prairie du Chien, Wisconsin.

Coal barges glide past on their way up the Mississippi toward La Crosse and on to Minneapolis. The townspeople lead generally wholesome Midwestern lives, and when Keith Govier was growing up, he went to church with his six brothers most Sundays of the year. The worst thing he ever did in high school was get caught riding in a stolen car one night. "I was on the edge of a bunch of questionable guys," he says with a shy smile. His blond hair and handsome appearance let you know that he couldn't have been much of a terror.

It was during his senior year that he and some friends walked to the front of the Wesleyan church during a revival meeting to make their professions of faith. "After that, some things definitely changed," Keith remembers. "I stopped swearing and running around and going to questionable places. Although I was following people's expectations to some degree, I had made at least a start to follow the Lord."

He worked a year after high school, then joined the Air Force, and by the age of nineteen had married his high school sweetheart. "Connie was Catholic, but she agreed to change over." When active military duty was finished, the young couple settled back in Prairie du Chien and worshiped regularly at first. Keith became a cop.

"I was working a lot of nights and weekends, and over the next three or four years, it was hard to get to church on Sunday morning. So she'd go on without me. Plus, in a town of only five thousand, the police know just about everybody's business. I found myself growing a bit cynical about church members to whose homes I'd be called to break up family arguments or drinking parties."

Old habits of speech and living began to return. Disagreements with Connie became more frequent, especially after a second pregnancy came along unplanned. Young Shawn had been one of the few delights of his life, but the thought of another newborn depressed him.

On the job, Keith would listen to his police partner tell about the various girlfriends he was enjoying. "Connie and I had waited for marriage," Keith says, "and I'd been faithful to her up to now, but I began to see what I was missing, and it looked appealing."

The turning point came in a discussion in the spring of 1979 when, after seven downhill years, Connie said she did not love him anymore. "That tore me apart," Keith remembers. "We had let a lot of problems build up unresolved, but that meant the end as far as I was concerned. If she didn't love me, I would find someone who did."

His affair over the next four months with the wife of a best friend brought physical pleasure, but it was not without misgivings. "I'd be alone in the patrol car at night, and I'd pray, 'Lord, I'm going to turn this all around. Please forgive me for what I've done. I'm going to stop.' The next morning, though, it was like I'd wake up, and Satan would say, 'You dummy, you know you can't do that.' And he was right."

Things came to a dramatic crisis when the woman decided to tell her husband she was leaving him. The news was suddenly all over town, and Keith felt he had no choice but to resign from the police force. His reputation had been smudged, and he had made himself all the more undesirable to Connie.

"But where was I going to find a new job in a small town?" He was soon on his way to Springfield, Illinois, to become a Montgomery Wards security manager. He set up an apartment, and when he called home after two months to ask how it was going, Connie's reply was "Fine—couldn't be better."

His lover, however, never took up his invitation to come to Springfield for a visit; she was earnestly trying to rebuild her own marriage. In time, Keith dated three local girls, the last of whom impressed him with her high standards. "Nancy wasn't a born-again Christian, but she was very organized and responsible—all the things that were missing in my life. It bothered me that she could be so moral without faith."

Gradually, something inside Keith told him, *You need to go back to church.* He did so several times, but held himself at a distance. "I felt lots of guilt," he says, "and I assumed I needed to straighten myself up first *before* returning to God."

His sister-in-law, concerned about what was happening and believing that Keith needed to be confronted, drove down from Madison, Wisconsin, to see him. Over a two-hour dinner she grilled him about his priorities, his responsibility for two young children, and the folly of trying to succeed apart from God.

"She was tough on me—but we'd always had a good

relationship, and I didn't resent her for what she said. I knew it was the truth. The trouble was, I was falling in love at the time, and I didn't want to give Nancy up.

"I couldn't make a decision. To be honest, I hadn't made any good decisions for a year. I'd just rolled with the punches as they came along, doing whatever was easiest at the moment. What I needed to realize was that indecision is a decision."

By December, Keith had been transferred to Niles, Ohio, a move that cooled the liaison back in Springfield. The financial noose was tightening around his neck as the cost of maintaining two households steadily drained his savings and forced the sale of such things as his boat. By the end of the month, word came from Wisconsin that a divorce suit has been filed.

"I was sitting alone in my bare apartment one winter afternoon with just a chair, a table, a TV, a bed, and not much else. I began watching a Christian program—I don't even remember which one. The longer I watched, the more I had to admit that I'd come to the end of the road. I knelt down and began to cry. 'Lord,' I prayed, 'here I am. I know I'm not much but a lot of trouble and a big stack of bills, but if you'll forgive me, you can use me however you like. I'm yours.'"

It was the beginning. An older woman at the Wards store referred Keith to a church in nearby Warren, where for the next four months "I grew spiritually more than ever before. They set me on my feet and pointed me in the right direction very quickly."

Could the marriage be repaired at this late date? He sat down and wrote a long letter, admitting the wrong he had done, asking Connie's forgiveness, and telling excitedly about the change in his life. Days passed, with no response. When he finally called, the answer was cool. "Well, I've heard all that before. You brought me out of the Catholic church in the first place, remember? But look what's happened in spite of your religion."

Keith continued to pray regularly for a restoration, right up until the court date in June. He could not afford a lawyer, but he drove to Wisconsin and met with her attorney, agreeing to what amounted to about an 80/20 split of the assets. At the trial, the judge asked him the crucial question: "Do you consider this marriage irretrievably broken?"

"No, Your Honor, I don't," Keith replied. "A lot of things have changed in my life, and I think we can put it back together again."

A look of shock came across Connie's face. When he stepped down from the stand, she stood and approached him. "You never said that before!" she whispered.

"Well, maybe not in those words, but that's really how I feel," he replied.

Nevertheless, by the time the judge put the same question to Connie, her response was firm. "Yes, it is broken; there's no chance for repair." And the divorce was granted.

Keith returned to his work; by this time he'd landed a better-paying position as security director of a large shopping mall in Rockford, Illinois. But "after about two weeks, it hit me. Why had I given in to everything so easily? Why had I taken on debts that should have been split 50/50? Why had I let her have the newer car while I drove the old junker, which was in desperate need of a valve job?

"I prayed not to feel animosity toward Connie. 'Lord, help me to stay away from the phone when I feel like telling her off.' After all, I was the one who cheated on her in the beginning, and her coldness toward my return to the Lord was understandable.

"The more I thought about my two kids growing up in a non-Christian environment, the more depressed I became. But the Lord seemed to assure me that he would meet my needs regardless. I kept reading the verse that had become real to me back in Ohio: 'Be strong and very courageous. Be careful to obey . . . do not turn from it to the right or to the left, that you may be successful wherever you go'" (Josh. 1:7).

God's kindness toward Keith was never more apparent than in the way his financial pressures were finally relieved. "We'd bought the house in Prairie du Chien through FHA, and after the divorce was final, their regulations required that the loan be rewritten in her name alone. The paperwork took a while to process, but when it was all said and done, I received a check for my half of the equity.

"Suddenly the load was gone. I cleared up all the old debts and was even able to trade cars with the surplus!"

Keith Govier's life today has stabilized; his bills are paid, his work is going well, and he's solidly involved in a growing church. When he leaves the mall in the late afternoons, he looks forward to spending time in the Scriptures. His pastor recently gave him a vote of confidence by asking him to work with the boys' club that meets on Wednesday nights.

The new era that has begun in his life is best expressed when he says, "I'm no longer a passive Christian. I want to learn more of the Word and to serve the Lord any way I can. The important thing in my life now is to concentrate on what will last."

The future is promising, not because Keith has done everything right in life so far, but because he's surrendered to the God who can handle imperfection.

The steps of a man are from the LORD . . .
   though he fall, he shall not be cast headlong,
for the LORD is the stay of his hand.

   Psalm 37:23–24 (RSV)

PART TWO
The Need for Confrontation

Facing Facts

An award-winning TV commercial for Alka-Seltzer once showed a middle-aged man in obvious distress after finishing off a large, well-topped pizza. As he clutched his middle, his wife stood by and reproachfully intoned, "You ate it, Ralph— you ate the *whole* thing."

Ralph could only stare into the camera and echo in a tomblike voice, "I can't believe I ate the whole thing."

There are times in our lives when we simply cannot find someone else to blame. We search the landscape in vain for another human being to indict. We say, "Well, it wasn't actually my fault, because . . ." and we can't finish the sentence.

In the past, we've been able to find alibis. There were circumstances that pushed us to do what we did. Older and more powerful persons misled us, gave us bad advice. Our problems were traceable to several sources, at least some of which were outside our control.

But this time, we can find no such cushioning. This is not a case of "It happened to me." This is a case of "I did it." We cannot sidestep the fact that the present predicament is of our own making, and to blame anyone else is but to prolong the self-deception.

We do not come to such an admission easily. It hurts too much. In fact, the various profiles in this book show that we often don't *come* to the ugly truth at all; we are dragged to it by outside forces. Circumstances gang up on us to such a degree that no other conclusion is possible; we must finally face the music. Only when the police move in, or a spouse explodes in enlightened rage, or the doctor confirms that a child is indeed on the way, must we grudgingly admit what has been going on.

What is sometimes hard for us to appreciate at this point is that there is more than just fate working against us. It is more than a matter of our luck running out. Behind the scenes, God is at work, quietly but irresistibly bringing us to his mirror. The events of our lives are his pressure bars, gradually nudging us where we would not go otherwise, until we are confronted with ourselves.

Why, after Jonah had rejected the instruction to go to Nineveh, did God not just let him proceed to a leisurely vacation in Tarshish? Jonah had made his decision; could not God move on to select another, more obedient prophet? Indeed, he could have done so, and with good justification.

But instead, he went to the bother of arranging a rather complicated set of phenomena. First "the LORD sent a great wind on the sea" (Jonah 1:4), and when that had sufficiently gotten Jonah's attention, "the LORD provided a great fish" (Jonah 1:17). The great wind and the great fish were effective; the prophet could no longer escape the fact that something was terribly wrong in his life.

The Book of Genesis tells us about Jacob spending all night trying to get ready for a critical meeting with his brother, Esau. Jacob has fought and scrapped to the point in life where he now has a growing family and flocks and herds, but his relationship with God is still sketchy. He comes to the Jabbok River and sends his caravan on across. Then in the darkness, all alone, he is accosted by a stranger.

They wrestle until daybreak, and when Jacob, exhausted,

asks for a blessing, the stranger asks an odd but penetrating question:

"What is your name?"

It is almost as if the divine messenger is saying, "Jacob, what is your real problem? You've blamed your father, Isaac, for his favoritism toward Esau; you've blamed your brother for his sour attitude; you've blamed your Uncle Laban for his shadiness—but down at the root of things, *who are you?* You're Jacob—the supplanter, the tricky one. Face it!"

And in that moment, God worked a fundamental change in Jacob's nature. He even gave the man a new name, Israel. His life from that night on had a different tone of sensitivity to his Lord, with the result that greater peace and happiness came his way.

Why does God force us to confront who we are and what we have done? Does he not know how painful it is for us? Does he enjoy embarrassing us, devastating our self-respect, watching us grovel in shame before him and everyone else who knows us?

Not at all. But God is wise enough to know that pain is the greatest motivator to change. It is a sad fact, but a true one. People change faster when they *hurt* than under almost any other condition. Any parent of a toddler will verify that sometimes words don't work; only a spanking gets the message through. It is not much different with adults.

More than thirty years ago the famous Lutheran speaker Walter A. Maier told his radio audience:

> This, then, is the purpose of pain for the redeemed: it is one of your Father's ways of speaking to you; it is the evidence of His limitless love, by which He would draw you farther from evil and closer to Him, the blessed means by which He would hold you back from sin, but hold you up to grace, the divine remedy which can cure you of pride and help you lean more trustingly on the Lord.[1]

So long as we do not perceive that we "really did eat the whole thing," so long as we are not aware of our willfulness, we are not likely to turn to the One who forgives and restores. God has a great fund of patience for us, but he will get to the bare facts eventually. "If we claim to be without sin," says 1 John

1:8, "we deceive ourselves and the truth is not in us."

Have you ever wondered why God dealt so harshly with Ananias and Sapphira in the early church, while other liars in the Bible (Abram and David, for example) seemed to get off much easier? Perhaps it was because Ananias and Sapphira refused to crumple when faced with the evidence; they kept up their pretension of righteousness even after Peter's question. They thus were an exhibit of Pharisaism, something Jesus hated almost more than anything else. He was determined not to let his church become infected with that virus. He stamped it out immediately.

In contrast, Jonah prayed honestly from inside the fish; Jacob admitted the kind of man he was; David poured out his heart in the Fifty-first Psalm and others. They yielded to the inexorable searchlight that bore down upon them.

One of the benefits of facing the facts is that we are then released from a great deal of tension. As Don Osgood notes in his book *Pressure Points*, "It reduces stress to admit we're wrong."[2] While our external dilemma may remain, our internal state has definitely improved. We know where we stand.

A woman who now works as an editor with a Christian publishing company tells of leaving home at the age of 16 to get married. She could hardly wait to escape the confines of her family and the negative church in her small town. She and her young husband set up their home a safe distance away, and two children were born in the first three years. But the rebellion within her kept surfacing, and the marriage soon split.

"Here I was, nineteen years old, with two kids to support," she says now from the vantage point of nearly three decades later. "I headed for the West Coast, blaming other people and other things for my troubles. But eventually I had to realize that *I* had made the choices. My life was a mess because of what I had elected to do with it."

She eventually remarried, began sending her children to Sunday school, and finally started going with them. By the age of twenty-four, her relationship with God had been repaired, and a useful adulthood was underway.

Alcoholics Anonymous has for years asked men and women to state that they have a problem out of control, a situation they cannot handle alone. Experience has shown that something crucial happens in that admission, something that unlocks the door to genuine change.

And change is what God is about in the end. He has no desire to fry us in the heat of exposure; he means to bring us to a new day. In fact, he may even have a surprise up his sleeve that will make positive use of our pain. The forty-year-old Moses, in a moment of outrage, committed murder. In that instant, his future as Pharaoh's protege was forever lost. He fled in terror to the Midian desert, there to contemplate the wreckage of his career.

But God began to restore him, and eventually commissioned him at a burning bush. His years of living in that rugged terrain were not a waste, for one day he would return to the same wilderness as the leader of a migration. His place of retreat would become his place of honor. The former murderer would become the man of God.

The unmasking of ourselves is a necessary part of God's process of healing. We must endure its pain and look forward to the relief that will surely follow.

For Your Reflection

1. Try to describe your life situation or difficulty using sentences that start with "I . . ." Reject any sentences that describe what other people or groups of people have done. Strive to name what is your responsibility.

2. Are there pressures forcing you to face reality, to lay aside the various explanations you've used in the past? What might God be trying to teach you through these pressures?

---

[1]Walter A. Maier, *He Will Abundantly Pardon* (St. Louis: Concordia, 1948), p. 76.

[2]Don Osgood, *Pressure Points* (Chappaqua, N.Y.: Christian Herald Books, 1978), p. 13.

PROFILE

The Pastor's Showdown

In this excerpt from his book Where Eagles Soar, *well-known author and speaker Jamie Buckingham describes how God painfully confronted him with a sin—not once but twice. He was a successful pastor in his mid-thirties at the time, but only after this canyon of embarrassment did his wider ministry as a writer emerge.*

Exposure comes, not for the sake of punishment, but for the sake of salvation. Fortunate is the man who is exposed early in life. Pity the man who is smart enough to hide his sin until the judgment.

Etched forever in my memory are the events that took place the night of exposure. Like Jacob at Peniel, I wrestled—and lost. October 1965. I sat in the beautiful conference room of that large Baptist church in South Carolina, surrounded by a group of 20 deacons, all with stern faces. They had tried over the last few months to convince me to resign. They knew something was wrong but until this dreadful night had found no evidence. As the months of suspicion continued, I hung on. To leave would mean admission of guilt. Worse, it would mean leaving behind a relationship in which I reveled with the same degree of intensity an alcoholic does with his bottle.

Twice before I had stood before the church at the monthly business meeting and gone through a "vote of confidence." Twice I had bluffed my way through. But this time there was concrete evidence. One of the deacons had discovered a note. I had been laid bare. My insides were churning. Desperately I tried to hold the façade of false confidence.

They asked me to leave the meeting and wait outside as they discussed the matter. Instead of at least a pretense at a sedate exit, I bolted. Fled. I stumbled into the darkened sanctuary and knelt at the front, weeping in fear and confusion. Back in the conference room the men were deciding my fate. In the next room was a small office. I called Jackie. "Come get me. I can't take it anymore." I hung up and in a state of near shock, shame and faced with the awfulness of it all, I wandered down a flight of stairs lit dimly by only the quiet redness of an exit light.

She found me, the shepherd of the flock, crouched in a fetal position in a basement hallway, huddled against the landing of the stairs. "It would be better for you, for the children, for this church if I were dead," I sobbed.

She comforted. She soothed. She never asked for details. There was no need. She led me by the hand through the dark hallways of the house of God to our car parked under the lighted window of the conference room. I did not realize it at the time, but those men were God's servants—sent by the Holy Spirit to perform the unpleasant task of shaking a man of God until only the unshakable remained.

That night I walked into the front yard of our beautiful parsonage. Standing under the autumn sky, I looked up into the heavens and screamed: "Take me! Take me now! Quickly!" In a desperate move, I grabbed my shirt and ripped it open at the chest, tearing the buttons and hem as I exposed my bare chest to the heavens, waiting for the inevitable flash of lightning which I knew would come and split me asunder, carrying me into the hell where I belonged.

But there was no flash of lightning, for the purging fire had already begun to burn. And besides, God does not punish sin the way we punish it. As ranchers burn off a pasture to kill the weeds so the new grass can sprout, so the consuming fire of God burns away the dross without consuming the sinner.

There was more to follow, of course. For one thing, we had to leave. Then there was the fear of going to sleep at night because I could not stand the thought of waking to a new day. Better to sit up sleepless nights than sleep and start a new day without trumpets in the morning. There was the desperate reaching out for friends, only to find they had all deserted. I was like a leper. Unclean. I wrote letters—more than 90 of them—to pastoral and denominational friends. Only one man dared respond and that was with a curt, "I received your letter and shall be praying for you."

Perhaps God was working here too; comfort or encouragement at that agonizing time could have moved me even deeper into a continuing self-deceiving sense of feeling justified.

And anyway, what else could anyone say?

We returned to my home state of Florida, to a small but rapidly growing church—the only opportunity that was open. But as Vance Havner once remarked, it doesn't do any good to change labels on an empty bottle. Nothing inside me had changed. I was still the magnificent manipulator, the master of control, the defender of my position. I was still pushing people around. I was far more politician than a man of God.

The Holy Spirit was not controlling my life.

Soon echoes from the past began drifting down to Florida—rumors of adultery, of manipulation, of lying. The old undertow of fear sucked at my guts. I was about to be swept back to sea for I had not been honest with the committee which had interviewed me for the Florida position. I could feel the insidious inevitability of confrontation creeping upon me again. I continued to fight, to brave the growing onslaught of fact that kept building the case against me. It took 15 months of a stormy relationship before the Florida church cast me into the waves to calm the sea—just like Jonah.

The crisis exploded one Sunday morning when I stepped up to the pulpit to preach. On the pulpit stand was a petition asking me to resign. It was signed by 350 people, many of whom were sitting, smiling, in the congregation. A group of men had hired a private detective and checked into my past. The detective's report—all 47 pages of badly distorted facts—had been duplicated and handed out to the congregation. The deacons demanded I take a lie detector test. Even though I passed it—declaring I had no intention of perpetrating upon that new church the sins of my past—it was not enough. I had no choice but once again to slink home and huddle with my wife and children while the fire of God continued its purging work.

Often, I have discovered, we cannot hear God when we are busy. Hearing comes only when we have taken—or are forced to take—times of quietness. With Moses it took 40 years of wandering in the burning sands of the Sinai, tending the sheep and goats of Jethro, his father-in-law and the priest of Midian, on the backside of the desert. It took that long for the fire of God to purge him of all the pride of his Egyptian prestige. Only then was he able to hear. Only then, when everything was quiet, did the angel of the Lord appear in the flame of fire out of the midst of the bush which burned but was not consumed. When a man has many things to do, he often does not have time to turn aside and see great sights. His time is consumed with busyness, his mind with activity. But Moses had time. So when the bush burned on the side of Mt. Horeb, he left his grazing flock and climbed the side of the rocky mountain to investigate. Then it was that God spoke to him and gave him direction.

So it was with me. All activity had ceased. No longer did I have to attend important committee meetings. No longer did I have to supervise budgets, direct visitation programs, promote an attendance campaign or even prepare sermons. All that I had felt was important was taken from me. There was nothing to do but tend the few sheep and goats who had pulled out of the church with me and were huddled together on the hillside grazing. I was beyond my own control. Then my bush burned.

* * *

Someone, perhaps my mother, had entered a subscription in my name for *Guideposts* magazine. I seldom read *Guideposts*, but in my idle time, which I now had in great abundance, I picked it up. Someplace in that particular issue I found a half-page announcement of a writers' workshop to be sponsored by the magazine. The stipulations were simple. Submit a first-person manuscript of 1,500 words following the basic *Guideposts'* style. This would be evaluated and judged by an editorial committee who would then pick the best 20 manuscripts. Those selected would receive an all-expense-paid trip to New York and would attend a one-week writers' workshop, conducted by the magazine editors, at the Wainwright House at Rye, New York, on Long Island Sound.

Several years before I had befriended a young man

who was preparing to go to South America as a missionary pilot with a group known as the Jungle Aviation and Radio Service, the flying arm of the Wycliffe Bible Translators. I had been intrigued with Tom Smoak's story. . . . Since I had nothing else to do, I wrote the story and sent it in.

My bush burned on October 1, 1967. I was stretched out on the bed in the back room of our little rented house when the phone rang. It was the Western Union telegraph office. Jackie took the call and copied the message on a scrap of paper. It was from Leonard LeSourd, editor of *Guideposts*, stating I was one of the 20 winners—out of more than 2,000 submissions.

. . . At the workshop John and Elizabeth Sherrill, both editors for *Guideposts* at the time, were approached by Dan Malachuk, a book publisher who was looking for a writer to compose the story of Nicky Cruz. Nicky was a former Puerto Rican gang leader from New York, now a Pentecostal preacher, whose conversion had played a major part in *The Cross and the Switchblade*, the book John and Elizabeth had written with David Wilkerson. The Sherrills were not interested in the project but recommended me. Before the week was out I had signed an agreement with the publisher and was on my way back to Egypt with a new sense of direction. I was going to become a writer. . . .

Perfection still eludes me. I am still vulnerable. But most important, I am no longer satisfied with my imperfection. Nor, thank God, am I intimidated by it. I have reached the point of recognizing that God uses imperfect, immoral, dishonest people. In fact, that's all there are these days. All the holy men seem to have gone off and died. There's no one left but us sinners to carry on the ministry.

Come, let us return to the LORD.
He has torn us to pieces
  but he will heal us;
he has injured us
  but he will bind up our wounds.
After two days he will revive us;
    on the third day he will restore us,
    that we may live in his presence.

  Hosea 6:1–2

Search me, O God, and know my heart;
    test me and know my anxious thoughts.
See if there is any offensive way in me,
    and lead me in the way everlasting.

  Psalm 139:23–24

What Do I Do
With the Memories?

When the blowtorch of exposure has finally turned away, we are left in a feverish state. The perspiration beads of memory stand thick upon our foreheads, adrenalin still speeds through our bloodstream, and we know it will be a long time before normalcy returns.

At such a time, we almost wish for amnesia. If only the past could be erased, if we could dismiss the pictures that flash in living color upon the screens of our minds. Instead, our misdeeds are rerun over and over, as if on a closed-loop film, from the beginning to the awful conclusion and back to the start. We force our brain to switch subjects, but before we know it, there we are again, thinking about it for the thousandth time. We identify with David, who, after his affair, wrote, "My sin is always before me" (Ps. 51:3).

Memory, we realize, is a two-edged sword; though it has served us well in the past, it now turns and threatens to destroy us. Memory is one of God's great gifts, a unique part of our creation as human beings in his image, but for the moment we would just as soon be a bit less gifted.

What do we do with our memories? There are several options available to us.

1. We can become their prisoner. The replay machinery of the brain has a vast power supply, and the tapes do not wear out with use; if anything, they become more indelible. It is thus altogether possible to live for weeks, months, and even years in a vicious trap of the past. What happened was quite possibly the greatest trauma of our lives; we had never been through anything like it before. The ordinary days that preceded it were not nearly so dramatic; we are now mesmerized by our days of infamy.

Emotionally, we ricochet from shame to anger to guilt to fear and back again. It is as if the four walls of the room have mottoes on them, and we carom from one to the next:

"What a fool I was!"

"God must be terribly angry with me."

"I wonder what people are saying now."

"The future is completely shot, isn't it?"

Round and round we go, from one anxiety to another, while the events themselves echo through our heads.

Dr. Haddon Robinson, a seminary president from Denver, has caught the intensity of this whirlpool in his contrast of two disciples, Peter and Judas. According to Matthew 26:75, Peter "went outside and wept bitterly." A few verses later, we read, "When Judas, who had betrayed him, saw that Jesus was condemned, he was seized with remorse. Then he went away and hanged himself" (Matt. 27:3, 5).

"Two broken men appear side by side on the stage of Scripture," notes Dr. Robinson. "When life overwhelmed one man, it marked his end, but for the other it was a place to begin again. . . . One came to the end of the line and demanded, 'Stop the world; I want off.' The second arrived at the end of the line and requested a transfer.

"For many men and women the agony of Judas and Peter becomes their own. . . . They arrive at a midnight moment. Hope disappears and they reach the end. Like Peter and Judas they face a choice—one that despair always offers—between remorse and repentance, between dying and weeping.

"While both men denied Jesus—in fact, betrayed him—

they did so for different reasons. Peter, it appears, denied Jesus because he did not want to die. Judas betrayed Jesus because he would not accept life as it is. He could not believe that for Jesus the path to glory led past a cross. In that sense, Judas was completely consistent. When he could not get life to suit him, he rejected it totally, completely, finally.

"Peter, on the other hand, stumbled through the worst weekend of his life until his risen Lord restored his hope and so changed him that the threat of death lost its power over him. Throughout the following years this same man risked his life to tell his countrymen the gospel of Christ."[1]

A second option, as time goes on, is even more deadly than the first.

2. *We can embellish our memories.* We can play with the dials as the tape moves along, heightening this, intensifying that, warping something else. While we are not likely to make major changes in the story, we can, over a period of time, remember the facts as even worse than they were.

Or, more commonly, we begin to place negative interpretations upon the facts. The reason we did such and such, we conclude, was that we're simply rotten individuals who always make a mess of things. All our vague misgivings and self-doubts link up with these events as proof of our worthlessness.

The next step of embellishment is to put ourselves on trial. Our memories serve as evidence of guilt, after which we act as judge to pass sentence upon ourselves. The married woman who had sex before her wedding night concludes that she must now deny herself any pleasure during physical union as a form of penance. The man who mismanaged his business into bankruptcy decides that he should be a day laborer from now on. Judas goes out to commit suicide.

3. *We can release our memories.* We can allow ourselves, with God's help, to lose track of some things! Although such behavior is not tolerated from computers, it is perfectly all right for humans. Our memory is *supposed* to be selective. The pain-

69

ful things are meant to recede over time, while the good things keep shining bright.

We smile at the widow who, as the months pass following her husband's death, speaks of him in increasingly glowing terms. When he was alive, she often complained and criticized, but now that he's gone, he was a saint.

Well, why not? Her memory is going through a sorting process, keeping the warm and beautiful while it discards the junk.

It is the Enemy who likes to hang on to the rubbish so he can keep using it against us. He enjoys exhuming it before our faces time and again, reminding us of how dreadful we were. He doesn't want us to release those memories, to forget.

In contrast, we see in Scripture the vivid example of the apostle Paul, who had enough nightmares in his past to paralyze him for life. He could close his eyes at any moment and see himself guarding a pile of coats while, a few yards away, the skull of Stephen was being smashed by flying rocks. He could remember a score or more of midnight raids on the homes of Christians . . . beating down doors, jerking men, women, and children out of bed, hauling them off to dungeons. He had terrorized a whole region, from Jerusalem to Damascus, until not a Christian was left who did not wince at the mention of his name.

Yet he rose to a height of apostleship that changed the Mediterranean world. How did he do it? Listen as he tells the Philippian church:

"Not that I . . . have already been made perfect, but I press on to take hold of that for which Christ Jesus took hold of me. Brothers, I do not consider myself yet to have taken hold of it. *But one thing I do: Forgetting what is behind* and straining toward what is ahead, I press on toward the goal to win the prize for which God has called me heavenward in Christ Jesus" (3:12–14, italics added).

Can you imagine how that must have thrilled the slave girl in the Philippian congregation who had given herself to demonic fortune-telling in the local marketplace until Paul came to town? Can you imagine its impact on the jailer, sitting a few rows farther back, as he contemplated the inmates he had almost certainly clubbed and maimed in years past? *Forgetting what is behind . . . straining toward what is ahead . . . press on.*

E. M. Blaiklock, the New Zealand scholar, says that the imagery behind Paul's words is a Roman chariot race, the kind most of us remember from *Ben Hur:*

> The charioteer stood on a tiny platform over sturdy wheels and axle. His knees were pressed against the curved rail, and his thighs flexed. He bent forward at the waist, stretching out hands and head over the horses' backs. This is surely what he [Paul] means by 'stretching out to the things before'. The reins were wound round the body, and braced on the reins the body formed a taut spring. It can easily be seen how completely the charioteer was at the mercy of his team's sure feet and his own fine driving skill. . . . In his intense preoccupation the driver dare not cast a glance at 'the things behind'. The roaring crowd, crying praise or blame, the racing of his rivals, all else had perforce to be forgotten. One object only could fill the driver's eye, the point to which he drove at the end of each lap.[2]

It is not our job to be sportswriters, analyzing the race for its flaws, its flukes, its missed opportunities, keeping a historical record. We are *in* the race, not up in the grandstand or the press box, and it is our job to push on to the finish.

What has happened in the past may not, in the end, be as important as *how we choose to feel and think* about what has happened. The way we choose to treat our memories has more to do with the future than the events themselves. If we are consumed with driving toward the goal Christ has held out for us, the past is not all that relevant.

Paul, writing to the seasoned believers at Ephesus (he had spent a full year and a half as their pastor), urged them to abandon the negative thought patterns of those around them, "to put off your old self . . . to be made new in the attitude of your minds; and to put on the new self, created to be like God in true righteousness and holiness" (4:22–24).

We have, in modern times, gotten a bad taste in our mouths

71

at the mention of words such as *holiness;* we immediately think about legalism and long lists of restrictions. We fail to remember that *holy* comes from the same root as *whole, health, heal,* and even *hale* (as in *hale and hearty*). Holiness is not legalism; holiness is healthiness. God intends to make us whole persons by calling us to take on new attitudes, future-oriented attitudes.

This does not happen overnight. The New Birth is not the total cure, but only the initial treatment in the process of bringing us to wholeness. Our return to God after a downfall is not a once-for-all miracle; it is rather a restarting of the change process toward emotional and spiritual health.

The important thing is not to stall at any point along the way, to quit the race. In the next segments of this book, we will probe in more detail how bad memories are released, the role of confession and forgiveness, and the return of equilibrium. In the familiar words of Hebrews 12:1, "Let us throw off everything that hinders . . . let us run with perseverance the race marked out for us."

For Your Reflection

1. Spend some time meditating on Ephesians 4:17–24. Notice especially the many references to mental states, attitudes, perceptions. What are the contrasts between verses 17–19 and 20–24?

2. In Philippians 3, how does Paul show his orientation toward the future? What differences do you think this made in his life and ministry?

3. When are you most plagued with recurring bad memories? What time of the day or week? On what occasions? How can you prepare to deal more firmly with those times of difficulty? If you plan ahead, what could be different next time?

---

[1]Haddon Robinson, "Focal Point" Newsletter (Denver: Conservative Baptist Theological Seminary, 1980).

[2]E. M. Blaiklock, *Cities of the New Testament* (Westwood, N.J.: Revell, 1965), pp. 43–44.

Fear not

Genesis 15:1; 21:17; 46:3
Exodus 14:13; 20:20
Numbers 14:9; 21:34
Deuteronomy 1:21; 3:2, 22; 20:3; 31:6, 8
Joshua 8:1; 10:8, 25
Judges 6:23
1 Samuel 12:20; 23:17
1 Kings 17:13
2 Kings 6:16
1 Chronicles 28:20
2 Chronicles 20:17
Isaiah 7:4; 35:4; 41:10, 13–14; 43:1, 5;
   44:2, 8; 51:7; 54:4, 14
Jeremiah 30:10; 46:27–28
Lamentations 3:57
Ezekiel 3:9
Daniel 10:12, 19
Joel 2:21
Zechariah 8:13, 15
Matthew 1:20; 10:26, 28, 31; 28:5
Luke 1:13, 30; 2:10; 5:10; 8:50; 12:7, 32
John 12:15
Acts 27:24
Hebrews 13:6
Revelation 1:17; 2:10

The Too-Soon Mother

"Yes, it's hard to look in the mirror sometimes and say, 'I'm a beautiful person God created.'" Eva Eber says with a touch of wistfulness in her soft brown eyes. Ryan, the preschooler to whom she is both mother and father, turns the pages of a Sesame Street book nearby, jabbering to his favorite Muppets.

"But the thing is, God cares enough about me to build me stronger through trials," she continues, her natural spark returning now. "Sometimes, when I have to discipline Ryan, it seems like the Lord whispers, 'That's how it is with you and me, too. I'm building character in you.' And I wouldn't want God to quit for anything."

The attractive young sales representative pours another cup of coffee and then leans back to recall the autumn she left Los Angeles at the age of nineteen to become a teacher's aide in a small desert town near the Nevada border. "I was tired of begging my parents to love me; I was tired of all the arguments, especially after I'd quit the Catholic church five years before. I was the first in our family to turn Protestant, and it caused endless fights. I had finally moved out, started college even while I was still finishing high school—and now I was at last on my own."

Her fondness for handicapped children found its fulfillment in the classroom. Meanwhile, she met a twenty-two-year-old Air Force sergeant at church. "He wanted to spend time with me, to listen to me, to give me acceptance," she says. "I told myself, 'You're lucky, Eva—if someone will honestly love you, take it and enjoy it.'

"When in November I took the final step, I never thought of what that could do to us. All I knew was that I loved him and wanted to give him more than just words. I thought this would build the warmth and security of our relationship.

"Well . . . I got pregnant the very first time. I was a little scared but more excited about having his child. I assumed we would just marry sooner than planned, and things would be great."

The sergeant took a far darker view of events. The fact that he was already a married man came out into the open, and he felt that the only option for Eva was abortion. When she refused, he became irate and threatening.

"Reality hit with a jolt," she remembers. "I was actually going to become a mother in the fall. My childhood image of a God of wrath ran wild in my head; my first response heavenward was 'Please don't beat me!' Soon I was mad—mad at the guy for deceiving me, mad at myself for going along with him, mad at everything.

"When I broke the news to my parents, I got another shot of condemnation about what a slut I was and how I'd never amount to anything. I wanted to remind them that I had been born 'early' in their married life, too, so who were they to talk? The chasm between us was awesome, and it was then that I moved in with my baby's father. I was scared to go it alone, and living with him was better than having no one at all."

As the hot summer wore on, her fears escalated. Visions of the children she had taught danced before her eyes. "God, you're probably just waiting to give me a deformed child, aren't you?" she snapped at one point.

But on September 15, when the doctor held up her strong baby boy and pronounced him perfect, Eva could not help weeping. "I was so wrong about God! I had assumed so many things that weren't true. He was showing me through Ryan that he still loved me in spite of the mess I'd created."

The presence of an infant in the apartment, however, brought added strain, and around the first of November, just as Eva returned to teaching, her lover moved out. Soon he had found a replacement, a seventeen-year old this time, whom he married as soon as his divorce was finalized.

"I was all alone now, and certainly not ready to be a single mother. Before I knew it, I was in deep debt. I had to get used to being the target of men's crude remarks. I struggled through the spring semester, and then came the final blow. Thanks to Proposition 13, my teaching job would be eliminated."

When school was out, Eva and her nine-month-old son moved to Riverside, California, where she managed a Wendy's fast-food outlet and began living the fast life. "I just went crazy—I dated everybody in sight," she says with regret. "I decided men were for using; all I wanted were arms to hold me through the night. A different man almost every night—it didn't matter. As long as they were footing the bill, taking me to clubs or out on their yachts, supplying the cocaine, keeping me from loneliness, that was all I wanted."

In case something drastic happened in this whirl, she took the precaution of making out a will. A girlfriend agreed to be named as Ryan's guardian. At one point Eva moved back to her parents' house to save money, but left again within weeks amid shouting and conflict. Shortly after Christmas, she narrowed her passions to one man, wealthy, divorced, father of three, twelve years her senior. "We were both hurting so badly that we got very dependent on each other quickly. We saw each other almost daily, and the relationship got very physical. But I wasn't about to get married, to give up my independence. Eventually, there was nowhere to go, and so we split.

"Deep inside, I knew I would eventually have to come back to God to break the destructive pattern of my life and keep from ruining Ryan along the way. I had had a good exposure to Christianity as a teen-ager; I'd gone to a Baptist camp with a friend and then kept attending the church that sponsored it. I'd gotten very active in special singing groups and even street witnessing. Christ had been a source of love and affirmation for me during those troubled years.

"So now, I went to church occasionally, looking for some of the peace I had known before. My lifestyle, however, mocked any seriousness that I may have pretended on Sunday morning."

In October, 1979, Eva and Ryan, now a two-year-old, left California for a short vacation with a Chicago friend. As the days passed, she sensed a great relief inside. Her accusing parents were two thousand miles away. Maybe she could start over here? She looked around for an apartment and a job.

Less than a month passed before she found herself in bed one night with her friend's former boyfriend. The next day she prayed, "God—just give up on me, why don't you? I've come halfway across the country, but things are still the same. I'm hopeless." Indeed, the same patterns persisted. "I kept bungling things, switching jobs, and hurting people. I was on a self-destruct groove, and I couldn't seem to break out."

By the following March, she literally had no place to live. A Christian girl she had met while working at a health club introduced her to an older woman, Eleanor Hill, who let Eva and Ryan move into her home temporarily. "I began to see a real Christian home for the first time. She guided me into the Scriptures once again.

"At one point, my mother flew out from L A, and we went together to see Eleanor's pastor. I cried out a lot of my fears in that session, like a little girl, while mom just listened. The result of that was a great reconciliation between us. She kept saying, 'I never realized . . . I never realized. . . .' We finally got to know each other, and I loved her because I wanted to for the first time."

By June she had a new job with a food broker. "The Lord began dealing heavily with me, forcing me to come to himself. I began a two-day fast. On the second afternoon, between sales calls, I pulled off the road to pray. A Scripture from Matthew 7 about people trying to enter the kingdom of heaven seemed to bear down upon me:

> Many will say to me on that day, "Lord, Lord, did we not prophesy in your name, and in your name drive out demons and perform many miracles?' Then I will tell them plainly, 'I never knew you. Away from me, you evildoers!"
> *Matthew* 7:22–23

"I was a Christian, wasn't I? I was going to church now, reading the Bible—in fact, I'd even counseled with a young pregnant girl recently, answering her questions about Scripture, trying to help her. What did this mean?

"It was as if God said to me, 'If someone has a need, I'll use whoever is around—even you. But that doesn't mean you yourself are right with me yet.'"

Eva contemplated that for four days, then returned

to the pastor with a question: "Is it possible that I'm not even a Christian?"

"Very much so," he replied. "That's why all your attempts at living as a Christian haven't worked. Even your Christian witness as a teen-ager back in California didn't guarantee that you were part of God's family."

Eva knelt and began to cry. Before the day was over, she had confessed her sins and asked for forgiveness. "I really wanted to receive Christ into the very center of my life. And I couldn't believe the relief when that happened!"

Peace came into her heart from that point. The confrontation had been worth it; her status as a child of God was finally established. In the days that followed, she began to sense God's guidance in various areas of her life that needed direction: handling money, dating, raising Ryan.

Even a severe bout of bronchial pneumonia combined with a heart condition later in the summer didn't devastate her. She was hospitalized several weeks; as a result, she lost her job and the company car that went with it. "But God was sustaining me. I was like a ceramic pot being put through the firing process. The first firing is the most crucial, when the pot can crack, the glaze can bubble, the paint can run. Those first few months were like that for me. But I survived.

"If anything, I had a problem at the first being too self-assured. I came on like 'I can handle everything now'—so much so that other people in my singles group were intimidated. I would never let on that anything was a problem in my life.

"The sickness and loss of job forced me to become more open and honest. I couldn't maintain the big front. I had to admit that I still had a lot of growing and trusting to do. I was out of work for a couple of months altogether, which tested me even further. But the words of Isaiah 43 became very precious during those days:

Forget the former things;
    do not dwell on the past.
See, I am doing a new thing!
    Now it springs up; do you not perceive it?
I am making a way in the desert
    and streams in the wasteland.
      Isaiah 43:18–19

That was exactly what was happening in my life."

In the late fall Eva began working again. In the time that has passed since then, her inward stability has mounted. "I sense a genuine distinction between myself and the world now," she says. "My co-workers notice it—they say things like, 'You don't get upset and cuss when things get hectic.' Also, I have the strength to tell men no. I believe God has a special person for me and for Ryan someday, but first I need to live by my standards for a while. God can't unfold the 'new thing' in my life until I have done some more maturing in him."

Eva knew she was making progress one night when her father called to ask for her help. "Your brother is really getting into a lot of trouble with drugs and everything," he said. "How about if I send him out to you? Take him to your church; talk to him. I know you can help him." Although, as it turned out, the brother was not sent, her father's warm expression of confidence was a welcome surprise.

Her attention for the time being belongs to her young son. "In a way," she says with a smile, "Ryan's presence makes me face responsibility and keep growing. Though we don't have a lot of material things and our apartment is a little bare in places, I'm learning how to live day by day with my Lord.

"He's taking care of me, remaking me into a person who honors him, and I'm satisfied."

I went down to the potter's house, and I saw him working at the wheel. But the pot he was shaping from the clay was marred in his hands; so the potter formed it into another pot, shaping it as seemed best to him.

Then the word of the Lord came to me: "O house of Israel, can I not do with you as this potter does?" declares the LORD. "Like clay in the hand of the potter, so are you in my hand."

Jeremiah 18:3—6

PROFILE

The Friendly Extortioner

Anyone reading the FBI files on Herman Heade, Jr., might naturally conclude that here is another typical slum criminal. Born and raised in Detroit's "Black Bottom" ghetto. Fathered a child while still a junior in high school. Two holdups and one bank extortion by the age of twenty-six. Nearly seven years of prison time altogether. An obvious loser.

What the record doesn't show, however, is that this handsome, athletic man started out with high promise. "My dad and I had a *good* home," he recalls with a smile, "and though he and my mom had split when I was four, she lived in the same part of the city with my two sisters. So we saw each other all the time, and we had a neat thing going."

The boy grew up with two loves: sports and school. His free time was spent playing baseball and reading. He stayed out of trouble on the streets, earning instead the B average necessary to get into Cass Technical High School, where he majored in performing arts. Every Sunday he was in church, singing in the choir, serving

85

as a junior deacon and also a Sunday school teacher. His father dreamed of getting him into West Point, while young Herman calculated his chances with the Detroit Tigers.

But before either of those could happen, a disagreement arose between father and son over the girl Herman had begun seeing. She was older and had a child. "Dad forbade me to keep on with her, and I resented it. So I did what I wanted. We had a son of our own by the time I was seventeen, and when I graduated from high school a year later, I quickly joined the Army to get away from my father's disapproval."

That November he finally married the young woman. He was soon sent to Vietnam, but after six and a half months, he received a hardship discharge because of the complications she was having in a new pregnancy. He came home with two medals on his uniform, "but I was a dead man, spiritually speaking. I thought my marriage would be stabilized now, but a fire seemed to rage inside me. I couldn't feel settled."

His job at North American Rockwell—the first black in the drafting department—did not satisfy him. Heavy drinking, the use of marijuana, and an assortment of women all became part of his weekly routine. When the cost of maintaining a seventeen-year-old girlfriend rose, he found himself in severe financial trouble. Bill collectors began calling the plant, and "one day I looked out the window to see GMAC towing away my car!"

Rather than change his lifestyle, he was obsessed with the question of how to get more cash. "I actually read the papers and watched TV to study how to pull off a robbery," he says now with amazement. "I left my wife and kids, invited my girlfriend to move into my new place with me, and then proceeded to hold up a cashier at the Montgomery Wards store where her mother worked. What did I get for my effort? Less than a hundred dollars."

The only thing to do was to try again. He bolstered his courage with liquor this time, pulled on a large hat, and walked into a bank brandishing a toy pistol. He handed the teller a note, and she produced twelve hundred dollars. "All those years in jail for such a little amount," he reflects with sadness.

The police had little trouble tracing him, and one night, he came out of a poolroom to find the parking lot strangely empty. It had been full when he entered just a couple of hours before. What had happened? As he stood staring, officers sprang up from everywhere. "There was a .44 Magnum pointed at my nose within seconds. My hands shot up—I was afraid they'd beat me. But they didn't. They just took me downtown and threw me in the drunk tank overnight, which was almost worse."

After thirty days of waiting in the Wayne County Jail, Herman was released on his own recognizance by both courts; the state court, which would try him for the Wards robbery, and the federal court, which held jurisdiction over crimes in federal banks. He continued to work for the next nine months until convicted and sentenced to five to fifteen years in Jackson State Prison for the first offense. The federal sentence of five-years-to-indeterminate would run concurrently.

"Jackson was packed with five thousand guys in those years, so I had plenty of 'instruction' about prison life. I spent seventeen months there, until the state supreme court overturned my conviction on a technicality. But that didn't set me free; it only meant I moved over to the federal institution at Milan, Michigan, to keep working on the other sentence. After another six months, I was paroled."

In the meantime, perhaps because of his outgoing personality and his way with words, he'd been invited to join a University of Michigan panel discussion on crime. There he had met the state corrections director, who now told him about a new experiment. The state was trying out a few ex-offenders as correctional officers, and Herman soon had a job at the Cassidy Lake Technical School for juveniles in nearby Chelsea.

"They may have thought I was reformed," says Herman, "but I jumped right back into living the old way again—TCP, Quaalude, grass, cocaine, and once again, obviously, I was needing lots of money. I couldn't support my lifestyle on my pay. When I'd go to see my kids in Detroit, I'd want to buy things for them, and I couldn't afford it."

He had been out of prison less than two years when he laid his plans for another robbery. This time he would not be so bold as to walk up to a stranger with a gun; instead he made an imitation bomb of cotton balls and wire inside a rolled-up newspaper, with a "fuse" sticking out that was actually a shoestring. He then sauntered into a Chelsea bank where a friend worked. He laid his little bundle along one wall, unnoticed.

"Hello, Frank, how ya doin', man?" he said as he slid into a chair beside the friend's desk.

"Doin' okay, Herman—good to see you. What's happenin'?"

Herman lowered his voice. "Say, Frank, you know what? I'm gonna rob you!"

Frank stared back. "What'd you say, man?"

"I said I'm gonna rob you. All you gotta do is go get me some money. See that thing over there by the wall? Go look at it, man—it's a bomb."

Frank nervously stood up, walked over to eye the odd-looking roll on the floor, and came back, his face taut. "Wow, Herman—well, at least don't light it till we get the customers out!" he whispered.

"Okay."

The tellers quickly cleared the lobby and then stuffed about six thousand dollars into an attaché case. Herman strode out of the bank and made for the Detroit airport, leaving Frank and the others to discover that they had been in no danger at all. By nightfall, Herman was in San Francisco, where he lived for the next three months, until loneliness and dwindling cash forced him, like the prodigal son, back to Michigan.

His welcome, however, was anything but warm. He approached his estranged wife's apartment under cover of dark. "Why did you do it?" she shrieked as soon as he walked in. After a few hostile minutes, he left. Fatigue pulled at his arms, his legs, his soul. He spent some of his few remaining dollars on a .32 automatic, then checked into a hotel. Sitting alone in his room, he seemed to hear a voice say: *Go ahead—pull the trigger. God will forgive you. Go ahead.*

Instead, he reached for the phone and called his father. "Well, son," the voice on the other end said, "if you're tired of running, I'll come be with you." Together they faced the fact that there was little else to do but call Herman's parole officer and turn himself in. Within hours he was back at Milan with a new charge of extortion, since the Chelsea robbery had involved the use of fear.

"I was placed in 'segregation' for the first ten months while I waited for trial, which meant only one hour a day out of my cell. During those long hours of thinking, I couldn't miss seeing how I'd cut off almost all my opportunities. I'd blown the chance to be a corrections officer; I'd ruined everything with my wife; I wouldn't be seeing my kids for another long spell now."

A group of segregated prisoners petitioned for a few privileges—access to telephones and to reading material. "One day during our free hour, a bunch of us were sitting out on some benches talking when the prison librarian walked up with a big bag. He dumped out a bunch of books, and we began eagerly sorting through them. I picked up one called *Peace with God* by Billy Graham and tossed it away.

"In a few minutes, another guy picked it up and said, 'Here, Herman, you ought to read this one.' For the second time I flipped it over my shoulder. I wasn't interested."

The second flip, however, happened to be in the direction of Herman's cell, where the book skidded along the floor next to the commode. "A few hours later, back in my cell, I discovered that book again! This time I opened it and began to read. The opening sentences hit me like a bolt:

> You started on the Great Quest the moment you were born. . . . Sometimes you have tried to forget about it. Sometimes you have attempted to lose yourself in other things so there could be time and thought for nothing but the business at hand. . . . But always you have been caught up in it again—always you have had to come back to your search.[1]

"I thought to myself, *Wow—he's right.* I kept reading. By page 139 I was bawling uncontrollably. But I was supremely happy inside, because I'd been born again while I was reading. It was like the chains came off my mind. I sat there saying, 'Praise God,' again and again.

"I finished the book and then spent the next two or three hours just thanking God for finding me, for giving me peace. It was incredible.

"I looked around my cell. I jumped up and began ripping down the pinup girls from the wall. The guy in the next cell looked through the bars and couldn't believe his eyes. 'What are you doin', man?' he wanted to know.

"'I've been changed,' I said. I tried to explain what had happened.

"He didn't really understand. I got the same reaction when I called my dad with the news—in fact, he cursed me out. My wife was cynical, too. Only my mother believed me."

Herman had difficulty getting a Bible through the prison bureaucracy, but that need was met when he was transferred to a new cell. There (he doesn't know how or why) a Bible had been left lying on the bed. He immediately sat down and read the New Testament straight through in six hours.

"But there were other guys in prison who had different ideas about the Bible. Being black, I got a lot of pressure to be a Muslim instead, and they would misinterpret the Bible as they tried to convince me to join them. I didn't know how to answer them. I vowed that I was going to learn somehow. I met with the Protestant chaplain, who explained to me about spiritual gifts. Was my gift exhortation? Maybe so, but I'd need some schooling before I would be worth very much, especially against the Black Muslims.

"Even they, however, couldn't deny the change in my life. The most obvious proof to everyone, and to myself as well, was that I cut out the dirty-joke telling. I'd been famous for my collection of stories, but now when the guys would call out, 'Hey, Herman—tell us some jokes!' I'd say, 'Sorry, guys. . . .'"

The psychiatrist who interviewed Herman prior to sentencing heard the full story of his conversion, more than an hour long. In court, the judge read the psychiatrist's report and then commented, "I don't understand." So Herman volunteered an on-the-spot testimony about the deep and permanent change that had taken place inside. When he finished, the room rang with applause.

The judge was impressed, but that did not deter him from imposing a new ten-year sentence for extortion, to be served at the federal penitentiary at Oxford, Wisconsin. Herman went to his new place looking for chances to learn more about his faith. He soon met a white employee named Donald Graves, a man in his fifties who led a Tuesday evening Bible study. "He adopted me as his son," Herman remembers with great admiration. "He taught me from the Word. He helped me enroll in the University of Wisconsin classes that were held in the prison, and he also got me connected to a couple of Christian correspondence schools. I began building a small theological library.

"Actually, some of my happiest days on earth were in Milan and Oxford as a new creature in Christ."

Herman continued to write letters to his wife back in Detroit, hoping to salvage the marriage. But in April, 1977, word arrived that a divorce had been processed. In June, 1978, he graduated with an associate in arts degree from the University of Wisconsin. And on September 27, after spending a full one-fifth of his life behind bars, he was paroled to a halfway house in Washington, D.C. He began working as a social assistant in a junior high school and was also soon speaking in churches, telling of the change he had experienced.

Since that time, he has moved into a full-fledged ministry. Today he is remarried, is the co-pastor of a Washington area church, and also works in prisons. He has led three-day training seminars in institutions all over the nation.

"The Christians will come," he says, "but then it's interesting how a lot of inmates who don't know Christ will wander in, too. What I have to say is good for both groups, actually: God hasn't forsaken you. Christ is the only answer to lift you up. And he can make all the difference in your future, if you want him to."

Remembering the people who helped him as an inmate, he now recruits Christian volunteers throughout Virginia, Maryland, and the District of Columbia to help him. Their efforts have been particularly targeted at Lorton Youth Center, where more than three hundred young offenders are kept.

"They listen to me," Herman says, "because I did so

much time myself. But they listen to all of us for another reason; we've got good news for them. One or two big mistakes don't have to ruin an entire life. There's a better way, for sure."

[1]Billy Graham, *Peace with God* (New York: Pocket Books, 1955), p. 3.

PART THREE
The Fruits of Confession

A Time to Speak

"I don't want to talk about it."

We have all used that phrase more than once in our lives, sometimes for better reasons than others. Unpleasant events large and small have been dismissed by it, or at least postponed for later handling. We have felt deep within us that words would only make matters worse, that we couldn't express ourselves accurately anyhow, or that we'd be taken out of context. The best policy, we concluded, was silence.

It is only natural in the wake of a major mistake that we should keep to ourselves for a period. That does not mean that we are at a standstill. Much of the progress outlined thus far—regaining our confidence in the God who rebuilds, meditating upon the Scriptures, facing the facts, dealing with our memories—must be inaudible. Nonetheless, we are a long way from where we started.

But perhaps there is a significance in the sequence of the immortal words in Ecclesiastes, "A time to be silent and a time to speak" (3:7). The Bible seems to indicate that after our initial stages of privacy, we must come to *verbalize* some things:

97

- The facts that we have already acknowledged in our heads
- God's view of those facts
- Our sorrow for what we have done
- Our desire to be forgiven and walk a different road in the future

Those words are what we call *confession:* the acknowledging in actual language of how things are.

* * *

If we are going to open our mouths at all on the subject, we had better start with talking to God. He is, after all, the one listener who will get it straight and not misinterpret us.

Listen to the prophet's call:

> Take words with you
>   and return to the LORD.
> Say to him:
>   "Forgive all our sins
> and receive us graciously,
>   that we may offer the fruit of our lips.
> Assyria cannot save us;
>   we will not mount war-horses.
> We will never again say 'Our gods'
>   to what our own hands have made,
>   for in you the fatherless find compassion."
> *Hosea* 14:2–3

And how does God respond to such candor?

> I will heal their waywardness
>   and love them freely,
>   for my anger has turned away from them.
> I will be like the dew to Israel;
>   he will blossom like a lily.
> *Hosea* 14:4–5

The call to confession rings throughout the Bible, from the patriarchs to the prophets to John the Baptist to the familiar words of 1 John 1:9 near the end—"If we confess our sins, he is faithful and just and will forgive us our sins and purify us from all unrighteousness." God knows we must do more than think about it; we must *say it* to him, in order that the issues of guilt and pardon can be clarified.

But what if we would "rather not"? Can we not just keep moving along toward restoration and wholeness without this embarrassment? The Thirty-second Psalm explains what happens if we try:

> When I kept silent,
> > my bones wasted away
> > through my groaning all day long.
> For day and night
> > your hand was heavy upon me;
> my strength was sapped
> > as in the heat of summer.
> Then I acknowledged my sin to you
> > and did not cover up my iniquity.
> I said, "I will confess
> > my transgressions to the LORD"—
> and you forgave
> > the guilt of my sin.
>
> Therefore let everyone who is godly pray to you
> > while you may be found.
> Do not be like the horse or the mule,
> > which have no understanding.
> *Psalm* 32:3–6, 9

There is no escaping the fact that confession implies a willingness to die. It is painful; it means giving up the old masquerade of okay-ness. It means admitting not only to ourselves but to a perfect God that we have blown it.

But let us not forget that on the far side of dying is resurrection. Confession is but a way station through which we pass en route to new life and health.

And in order for God to bring us to that destination, he sometimes requires us to repair the relationships we have damaged with other people. We must talk not only to God in heaven; we must summon the courage and humility to talk to certain individuals here on earth. If, for example, our husband or wife is to be a part of God's bright future for us, we cannot enter that future without dealing with the hurts we may have inflicted. Confession is not only vertical; it is horizontal.

We shrink from such honesty for the same reasons that we hesitated to come to God—and for some other reasons as well. We don't know whether our confession will be accepted or turned down; we fear an attack of blame instead of a welcoming spirit. In some cases we rationalize, "What they don't know won't hurt them," refusing all the while to admit that what they don't know is killing *us*, festering inside, poisoning all attempts at sincere dialogue. The days and weeks pass along in a haze of playacting; only a brave act of confession will clear the air.

When the prodigal son in Jesus' story thought about going home, he knew he would need to do more than just walk through the front door. *He would have to say something.* He planned his sentences even while in the pigpen: "I will set out and go back to my father and say to him: Father, I have sinned against heaven and against you. I am no longer worthy to be called your son; make me like one of your hired men" (Luke 15:18–19).

As it turned out, he got only partway through his speech before his ecstatic father cut him off with the order for the best robe, the ring, and the fattened calf. Nevertheless, the words were important. They crystallized, for the son most of all, the dramatic turnaround in his life. It is often the same with us. God and the people we have offended need to hear us say it—but more than they, we need to hear ourselves say it. It is then a matter of record, a fact of a certain day, time, and location that we can recall for the rest of our lives.

One person, after an excruciating public acknowledgment of his fall, looked back and said, "If there had been no confession, there would have been no chance for the people of God to respond to me. They would simply have had to wait in silence, wondering. But as soon as I spoke—hard as it was to do—it released them to reach out in love and forgiveness. The healing process could begin."

In response to our definitive statements, God makes a few proclamations of his own. The Scriptures are full of his promises to forgive completely, utterly, irrevocably. While some people may struggle with whether to write off the past, God does not. He forgives totally; if he didn't, he wouldn't be God.

Fallen Christians are sometimes not sure about this. Can God really forgive as completely now as when we first came to him for salvation? Doesn't he keep some sort of black list?

"I will forgive their wickedness," God announced through Jeremiah after about a thousand years of Israel's ups and downs, "and will remember their sins no more" (31:34).

David claimed in Psalm 103:12 that our transgressions are removed "as far as the east is from the west." Anyone who has ever flown from New York to New Delhi, or from Tokyo to Tel Aviv, can appreciate that.

Ephesians 1:7–8 explains why God grants such a clean slate. Our forgiveness, technically, is not ours; it is Christ's! *"In him* we have redemption through his blood, the forgiveness of sins, in accordance with the riches of God's grace that he lavished on us with all wisdom and understanding" (italics added).

What does it mean to be "in Christ"? This common New Testament expression is well illustrated by Bruce Narramore and Bill Counts in their book, *Freedom from Guilt:*

> Suppose you put a piece of paper between the pages of a book, then close the book. Whatever happens to the book happens to the paper. If you throw the book away, you throw the paper away. If you put the book in a safe place, you safeguard the paper. If the paper is dirty and spotted, you don't see the dirt at all—you only see the book. The same is true of our position in Christ. When God looks on us, He sees us "in Christ." He doesn't see our dirt. He sees us just as clean and pure as Jesus Christ himself.[1]

Do we *feel* forgiven and restored after confession to God? It doesn't matter. The fact is, we are. We are in Christ, and that is enough.

Gwynn Lewis, a young Ohioan who ruined his life with drugs and eventually set up a drug dealing operation in Ecuador, was finally arrested along with his live-in girlfriend. He spent months rotting in a rat-infested prison, until a missionary began to visit him and eventually led him to faith in Christ. The missionary also helped get him released and back to the United States. On the next-to-last page of his short book, *Nightmare in Paradise*, Lewis says:

> People sometimes ask me if I feel any guilt or remorse for my former life. The answer to that is *absolutely not!* I have been forgiven; I *feel* forgiven totally and completely. I am a new person. Part of that feeling is due to Jerry Reed, I'm sure. He treated me like a new man even before I was. Never once did he hold back; the love and respect I felt from him were genuine, and better than I probably deserved. From him I learned something of God's grace, and that goes a long way towards erasing any guilt that might have lingered.[2]

The full sweep of repentance and restoration can be seen in the second chapter of Joel's prophecy in the Old Testament—a beautiful outline of God's plan for tripped-up people. The nation has fallen into serious sin, but here, in what might be called the Bible's Comeback Chapter, are four important events:

1. The Punishment (vv. 1–11). Sin and backsliding bring, in this case, an invasion of locusts that strip the countryside of everything green.

> they leap over the mountaintops,
> like a crackling fire consuming stubble,
> like a mighty army drawn up for battle.
> They climb into the houses;
> like thieves they enter through the windows.
> It is dreadful.
> Who can endure it?
> *Joel 2:5, 9, 11*

The point is clear: sin has consequence. We do not get away with things that displease God. But then—

2. The Repentance (vv. 12–17). People who have been dev-
astated have an option after all. They do not have to simply go
on suffering.

> "Even now," declares the LORD,
>> "return to me with all your heart,
>> with fasting and weeping and mourning."
>
> Rend your heart
>> and not your garments.
> Return to the LORD your God,
>> for he is gracious and compassionate,
> slow to anger and abounding in love,
>> and he relents from sending calamity.
> Who knows but that he may turn and have pity
>> and leave behind a blessing—
>> *Joel* 2:12–14

And what will be the result of this confession? Will it do
any good?

3. The Restoration (vv. 18–27). The passage begins with the
pivotal word "Then" and proceeds to tell all that God will do.
The "northern army" will be pushed out; the land will again
produce crops; rainfall will return; the threshing floors will be
filled. And then comes an almost incredible bonus, far beyond
what we deserve:

> "I will repay you for the years the locusts have eaten—
>> the great locust and the young locust,
>> the other locusts and the locust swarm—
> my great army that I sent among you.
> You will have plenty to eat, until you are full,
>> and you will praise the name of the LORD your God
>> who has worked wonders for you;
> never again will my people be shamed."
>> *Joel* 2:25–26

It would be enough to gain relief from the pressures we
brought upon ourselves. But to be repaid for lost time is almost
unfathomable.

103

The Comeback Chapter concludes with a glimpse of . . .

4. *The New Usefulness (vv. 28–32).*

> "And afterward,
>> I will pour out my Spirit on all people.
> Your sons and daughters will prophesy,
>> your old men will dream dreams,
>> your young men will see visions.
> There will be deliverance,
>> as the LORD has said,
> among the survivors
>> whom the LORD calls"
> *Joel* 2:28, 32

This prophecy was fulfilled specifically on the Day of Pentecost, but as Peter explained to the curious crowd that day, "The promise is for you and your children and for all who are far off—for all whom the Lord our God will call" (Acts 2:39). We must not limit the words of Joel to one event of history; God is still in the business of pouring out his Spirit on repentant people, causing those who have wrecked their dreams to dream new ones, showing wonders not only in the heavens but also on the earth—in the lives of "the survivors."

But in our eager yearning for stages 3 and 4, we cannot by-pass stage 2. The "Then" of Joel 2:18 and 27 must necessarily follow the "Even now" of verse 12. The fireworks of verses 28–32 begin with "And afterward. . . ." Confession and repentance are the keys that unlock the door to God's favor, and there are apparently no side entrances.

For Your Reflection

1. Study the Comeback Chapter (Joel 2) for yourself, marking the four sections in the margins of your Bible, and noting the progression from one to the next.

2. Do you tense up at the thought of actually blurting out your confession to God? Use Daniel 9:4–19 as a model for praying. Notice how honest Daniel is, how willing to "put all

the cards on the table." After you've read the passage, take a sheet of paper and write your own paraphrase, based on your own personal situation. (Daniel's forthrightness, by the way, resulted in a visit from no less than the angel Gabriel—see the rest of the chapter.)

3. If you're still not sure whether God forgives and restores adulterers, robbers, cheats, and other scoundrels, see Ezekiel 18:10–13, 21–23, 27–28.

4. Begin praying for the inner strength to clear the air with the people you've wronged. Then follow through; do your part to answer your own prayer.

---

[1]Bruce Narramore and Bill Counts, *Freedom from Guilt* (Irvine, Calif.: Harvest House, 1974), p. 81.

[2]Gwynn Lewis, *Nightmare in Paradise* (Old Tappan, N.J.: Spire, 1978), p. 94.

PROFILE

The Haunted Wife

Dr. Richard D. Dobbins, a veteran of more than twenty-five years in the pastorate, now heads an Akron-based counseling and mental health ministry. He travels widely to speak on how personal wholeness can be gained through spiritual avenues. On one of his cassettes entitled "The Healing of Memories," he tells the following story of a woman he refers to as "Evelyn."

* * *

She grew up in an Assembly of God church; her father was a board member. During her teen years she dated the president of the youth group, and they prematurely committed themselves to each other. She became pregnant.

At six months in her pregnancy, the people of that church put pressure on the pastor to dismiss her father from the board. They also moved to force her and the youth president to stand up on Sunday morning and confess that they had done something wrong.

We hurt when we hear things like that, don't we? And yet these things were done in the name of keeping the church clean.

Needless to say, the wounds were deep and raw and ugly and open. Miracle of miracles, both of them stayed in the church. It wasn't easy, but they lived it down. . . .

Now, at forty-some years of age, she was sitting in my office. In the first two sessions, she commented, "There's something I need to talk to you about—but I'm afraid if you know, you'll never have any respect for me."

What I didn't know then was that one of the teen-agers in the church who had been her friend when all of this happened, who knew all of the sordid details, had moved away—and now, after twenty-some years, was moving back.

And in Evelyn's mind, *time stood still.* She and her friend were teen-agers again, and she was threatened with great fear that this woman was coming back to begin the story all over.

In our third session together, Evelyn told me her past. She had never really dealt with it before. It had been there, like a raw abrasive in her marriage. She couldn't have right feelings toward her husband, because she wasn't sure whether he had married her because he loved her or because he had to. He had told her a hundred times or more that he had married her because of love. But the emotional blockage just would not let the message come through.

I will never forget the day when she began to weep convulsively in my office, and I said to her, "Evelyn . . . have you asked the Lord to forgive you of this?"

"Ho!" she said. "Have I asked the Lord to forgive me? I've asked him a hundred times!"

"Well . . . do you believe he has?"

"Oh, yes, I believe the Lord has forgiven me—but how can I forgive myself?"

And then I said quietly and slowly, "Oh . . . are you

holier than God is?" I paused. "Must God sacrifice *another* Son just for the sake of your conscience?" Another pause. "If the death of Christ was good enough for God, isn't it good enough for you?"

It is hard for me to describe the beautiful scene that transpired as the Holy Spirit pressed that truth to her heart. She broke down and wept for ten minutes or more. The expression on her countenance when she finished weeping was obviously changed. After we prayed to end our session that day, she said, "This is the first time in over twenty years that I feel no condemnation."

Jesus died that the people of God might never suffer from guilt or fear. "If we confess our sins, he is faithful and just to forgive us our sins, and to cleanse us from *all* unrighteousness."

Free Indeed

When we speak of confession and forgiveness, we often worry about two extremes: making it all too easy, and making it all too hard. On the one hand, is it really so simple as a mere "I'm sorry"? Surely we must agonize more than that. But on the other hand, would all of our agonizing turn the trick in the end? King Henry IV of Germany was once kept waiting barefoot in the Alpine snow for three January days before the pope would forgive him. Was that really necessary? Does not Jesus invite us to come simply and accept the atonement he won on the cross?

Dr. Richard Dobbins, the pastor-psychologist mentioned earlier, has built a helpful model of the dynamics at work in processing guilt or regret.[1] He grew up in a wing of Protestantism that urged people carrying spiritual burdens to do what was rather quaintly called "praying through." By that the old-timers meant more than just talking to God with head bowed; they meant staying at the altar of the church and working through the issues in prayer until a sense of release finally came. It might take an hour or longer; it might even require several sessions. But in the end, the time was well spent.

Dobbins suggests that "praying through" was more than

just a quirk of Bible Belt revivalism. His clients now use it, in fact, as a form of self-help between counseling sessions. The process has four steps:

1. *Name the damage intellectually.* Tell God what actually happened. Identify the source of the current pain.

As has already been discussed, this is sometimes hard to do. We don't want to be this honest. But in the presence of a Father who loves us and has promised not to evict us, we are safe.

2. *Allow our feelings about what has happened to come to the surface and flush out.* We may have repressed our anger, self-hatred, or disappointment for a long time, but we can only get rid of such emotions by emptying them. Our destructive thought patterns will never change until we express them, preferably alone to God. If this is accompanied by crying or other kinds of outbursts, we need not be embarrassed. The emotional reality is as serious as the objective reality.

At the end of this phase, we have a sense of great relief. This is the time "when the burden lifts," as some have called it.

But we are not finished. We need more than just a ventilation of tension.

3. *Meditate; let the Word and the Holy Spirit show how our old perceptions have been hurting us, and wait for a new meaning or interpretation of the facts.* As Hebrews 4:12 says, "The word of God is living and active. Sharper than any double-edged sword, it penetrates even to dividing soul and spirit, joints and marrow; it judges the thoughts and attitudes of the heart." If we are willing to spend portions of our prayer time listening rather than talking, we will find God shedding new light on our circumstance. He will move us past our mistake; we will hear ourselves saying, "At least now I know some of the worst things about myself. I can't be fooled that way again!"

And as we wait in God's presence, we become aware of

options for our future. We are released from our first fixation on the tragedy; we find less painful ways of thinking about our lives.

4. *Replace the old, hurtful interpretations with the new ones gained through meditation and prayer.* We can lay aside the thoughts that have been jabbing at us as we take up the divine perspectives. We can even begin to praise God for the relief he has granted and the new meaning he has given to the event.

"Writing down the new way of looking at the old hurt often helps to fix it in your mind," says Dobbins. "If you even add the date of your experience of relief, you can then remind yourself when tempted to pick up the old hurt again."

An example: Imagine a woman whose pregnancy was unintended. She is now suffering from post-natal depression. The fact of the baby's presence is clear enough (step one). In step two, she may go ahead and articulate her anger at herself and/or her husband for not using proper birth control methods. She may also say that she feels terribly wicked for resenting this beautiful, innocent child. She admits to the Lord that she is, so far, a begrudging parent.

But as she meditates, some new ideas come to the surface. Her career plans are not dashed forever. She can resume her work outside the home in a few years. Things are perhaps not as bad as she first thought. She eventually takes up mothering as a valid and rewarding part of her life.

Several writers and teachers in the area of inner healing have outlined similar steps to "praying through." They lead hurting people through an imaginary replay of past traumas—only this time, the person visualizes Jesus in each scene, healing, soothing, binding up wounds, placing new interpretations on all that happened.

Narramore and Counts explain the benefits of what they term "constructive sorrow"—something sharply different from "psychological guilt," or self-condemnation. The contrast is clear in Paul's comments to the Corinthian church:

113

> Even if I caused you sorrow by my letter, I do not regret it. . . . For you became sorrowful as God intended and so were not harmed in any way by us. Godly sorrow brings repentance that leads to salvation and leaves no regret, but worldly sorrow brings death.
>
> *2 Corinthians 7:8–10*

The difference, say the co-authors, is that "psychological guilt produces self-inflicted misery. Constructive sorrow produces a positive change of behavior."[2]

> David's full confession, recorded in Psalm 51, reflects both psychological guilt and constructive sorrow. If David had immediately repented over his sins, he would have avoided much psychological guilt. But the long delay, compounded by further deception, loneliness, and David's own psychological makeup programmed him for destructive guilt. . . .
>
> Psychological guilt helped keep David in spiritual paralysis for a year! Constructive sorrow brought him immediate repentance and release.[3]

Call it whatever you like—the process of confession and forgiveness is a strategic part of starting again. And experience has shown *we usually need more than one time through the process* before we are fully restored. Dobbins notes that people sometimes need to recycle even fifteen or twenty times as they gradually lay to rest various segments of their inner pain. "The trouble is, many Christians get through praying before they've 'prayed through,'" he quips. "We have all seen the plaques that read, 'Prayer changes things.' It's my observation that prayer usually changes people, and people change things."

In an age that calls for instant fixes, we are not always patient with such a gradual approach. We would do well to heed the oriental proverb, "Don't push the river." The stream of God's grace will carry us where we need to go; our thrashing about will only exhaust us. When we find ourselves like Joseph in a pit of calamity, we too often pray for a helicopter evacuation rather than wait to be made ruler of all Egypt in time.

Our task is rather to cooperate with the process, to continue confessing our wrongs and our destructive attitudes as we become aware of them, and to receive the Holy Spirit's new interpretations in return. Hebrews 12 exhorts us not to resist God's disciplining work; it is a sign that he takes us seriously. "No discipline seems pleasant at the time, but painful. Later on, however, it produces a harvest of righteousness and peace for those who have been trained by it" (v. 11).

How will we know that we are whole again? Some signs that the process is reaching completion are:

- *When we can thank God for the lessons learned through the ordeal.* Our new insights have shown us that we are better, wiser Christians now, and we are grateful.

- *When we can talk about what happened without getting upset.* When the subject comes up, either in general or specifics, we can handle it. We no longer turn red, hold our breath, or leave the room. When the pastor mentions the name of "our" sin or shortcoming from the pulpit, we don't flinch. We have been thoroughly forgiven.

- *When we can revisit the scene or the people involved without getting upset.* Granted, it may not always be wise to go back to a certain town or ring a certain doorbell, for the shock that other people might experience. But for ourselves, we have the capacity to do so without falling to pieces. God has swept the shame and guilt out of our consciousness, and we are free indeed.

The way of confession and forgiveness is neither too easy nor too hard. It brings us to terms with God, and it sets us in the end on a new and promising course. It releases us to enter a future of brightness and hope.

For Your Reflection

Engage in several episodes of "praying through," using the four steps outlined in this chapter. Use the following Scriptures for meditation, or others to which the Holy Spirit directs you.

- Psalm 51
- Jeremiah 31
- James 1

[1]Richard D. Dobbins, "The Psychological Benefits of Sanctification" cassette with notes (Akron: Emerge Ministries, 1979).
[2]Narramore and Counts, *Freedom from Guilt*, p. 124.
[3]Ibid., p. 131.

PROFILE

Diary of an Adulterer

In his book Let Us Enjoy Forgiveness, *Judson Cornwall explains and then illustrates how completely God removes our sins once they are confessed. This excerpt begins with a comment on Colossians 2:13–14, "He forgave us all our sins, having canceled the written code, with its regulations, that was against us and that stood opposed to us; he took it away, nailing it to his cross."*

The more common Greek word for the cancellation of a contract is *chiazein*, which means to write the Greek letter *chi*, which is the same shape as a capital X, right across the document. This was called a "cross out." But Paul uses the Greek word *exaleiphein*, which literally means "to wash over," as in whitewashing, or "to wipe out." The ink used in Paul's day was basically soot mixed with gum and diluted with water. It would last for a long time and retain its color, but a wet sponge passed over the surface of the papyrus could wash the paper as clean as it had been before the writing had been inscribed on it. This is the word Paul uses here.

117

Our sins have not merely been canceled out; they have been blotted out. . . .

God made this truth tremendously clear to me when I was pastoring on the West Coast. I had been burdened for a pastor who had been defrocked by his denomination for immorality and had moved to my community to start life over as a watchman for a plywood mill. Over a period of many months, we lunched together and came to know each other quite well. I continuously sought to cause him to accept the forgiveness he used to preach and encouraged him to live as a forgiven man, but it was difficult for him, since he had lived most of his life in the concept that God has a separate standard for ministers. After more than a year, the reality of God's forgiveness began to dawn upon him. He and his wife attended our church, and he occasionally ministered for me. It was great to see this guilt-ridden brother begin to accept the fullness of God's glorious forgiveness. In time, his denomination recognized the change in him and reinstated him, offering him a small church to begin his ministry anew.

The day he was to leave to accept this new charge, I phoned him on his job to assure him of my continued interest and prayers, only to be informed that he had changed his mind.

"Why?" I inquired. "I thought it was all settled."

"Judson," he said, "I just can't go through with it. After what I did in my last church, I don't deserve another chance. I'm not worthy to preach the Gospel of Christ anymore."

Shocked and disgusted, I hung up on him and went directly to the prayer room in the church.

"Lord," I prayed, "have I been mistaken about him all along? Did he really confess his sin, or did he merely admit his guilt? Is he caught up in self-condemnation, or is he still guilty in your sight?"

God's answer came in the form of an immediate

vision. With my eyes still closed in prayer, I saw myself in a large room that had bookcases on all four walls with volumes of leather-bound books from floor to ceiling. It reminded me of a legal library. As I looked at the books, I saw that they were alphabetized by names of people. A large hand with an extended index finger began to move across the books, until it came to the one with this minister's name on it. The book was removed from the shelf, placed on a small table, and opened in such a way that I could see and read the pages. The first page told the story of his birth, and subsequent pages told of his early childhood, of his call into the ministry while he was still in his teens, of his first ministry and pastorate, of his courtship and marriage, and of his climb to a respected position in his denomination. I could only wish I possessed the ability to read as rapidly in real life as I was able to read in that vision. Everything that I read fit what I had come to know about this man.

The top of each page was dated, very much like a diary, and as the pages got closer and closer to the first incidence of adultery, I wondered how God would have it recorded. But when the book opened to that date, the page was absolutely blank, as were succeeding pages for what would be chapters of space. Then when we came to the date of his repentance, it was fully recorded with a marginal gloss that this had produced great rejoicing in heaven. Following this, the pages recorded his progress back into faith, his ministry in our church, his reacceptance into the denomination, and his call to the new church. Puzzled by the many blank pages, I asked if I could have a closer look at them. My request was granted, and I saw that there had been writing on the pages, but that it had been erased. On the bottom of each erased page, in red, were the initials "JC."

True to his word, Jesus Christ had "blotted out the charges proved against you, the list of his commandments which you had not obeyed" (Colossians

2:14 LB). Heaven had no record of this man's sin. The only existing record was in his memory.

Excited with this revelation, I rushed to the phone and called the brother. After I told him what God had shown me, he quit his job, took the church, and re-entered the ministry as a forgiven man.

God does not forgive and then file it away for future reference; He forgives and then erases the record. The pages of transcript that record our sinning are erased clean. Even the tape recording of our confession is erased, so that none will ever have access to our past. The guilt is removed and so is the evidence. This is the way God forgives the repentant one. Acts 3:19 urges us, "Repent ye therefore, and be converted, that your sins may be blotted out [Greek *exaleiphein*], when the times of refreshing shall come from the presence of the Lord" (KJV).

PART FOUR
Moving On

It's Only Halftime

On New Year's Day, 1919, Georgia Tech played University of California in the Rose Bowl. Shortly before halftime, a man named Roy Riegels recovered a fumble for California. Somehow he became confused and started running—sixty-five yards in the wrong direction. One of his teammates, Benny Lom, outdistanced him and downed him just before he would have scored for the opposing team. When California attempted to punt, Tech blocked the kick and scored a safety.

The men filed off the field and went into the dressing room. They sat down on the benches and on the floor, all but Riegels. He put his blanket around his shoulders, sat down in a corner, put his face in his hands, and cried like a baby.

If you have played football, you know that a coach usually has a great deal to say to his team during halftime. That day Coach Nibbs Price was quiet. No doubt he was trying to decide what to do with Riegels.

The timekeeper came in and announced that there were three minutes before playing time. Coach Price looked at the team and said simply, "Men, the same team that played the first half will start the second."

The players got up and started out, all but Riegels. He did not budge. The coach looked back and called to him again; still he didn't move.

Coach Price went over to where Riegels sat and said, "Roy, didn't you hear me? The same team that played the first half will start the second."

Roy Riegels looked up, and his cheeks were wet with a strong man's tears. "Coach," he said, "I can't do it. I've ruined you; I've ruined the University of California; I've ruined myself. I couldn't face that crowd in the stadium to save my life."

Coach Price reached out and put his hand on Riegels's shoulder and said to him, "Roy, get up and go on back; the game is only half over."

Roy Riegels went back, and those Tech men will tell you that they have never seen a man play football as Roy Riegels played that second half. . . .

We take the ball and run in the wrong direction; we stumble and fall and are so ashamed of ourselves that we never want to try again, and He comes to us and bends over us in the person of His Son and says, "Get up and go on back; the game is only half over."

—Haddon W. Robinson

New Things

To be forgiven, to have our blot erased and forgotten, is a great gift.

But to watch God fill the empty space, writing a new thing upon the tablet of our lives, is even greater.

It is the final evidence that he does not hold a grudge, that he has not schemed some kind of residual punishment for us. His love is so complete that it does not stop until he has assured us that we are more than just tolerable in his sight; we are valuable.

Why do we remember Abraham as such a notable man? Because of what God did with him *after* he bolted away from God's plan for his life. He had followed the call to migrate to Canaan, but almost immediately he left. "Now there was a famine in the land, and Abram went down to Egypt to live there for a while because the famine was severe" (Gen. 12:10).

In Egypt, one problem followed another. He began to fear for the safety of his attractive wife. So he plotted with her to lie about their relationship. Sarai was indeed taken into the royal harem for a time. Finally the Lord had to intervene with a plague, which exposed the facts and got Abram expelled from the country with all his caravan.

And that was not all. Somewhere in the process they picked up an Egyptian domestic named Hagar, who proved to be the source of later contention that almost split the marriage. The world today, in fact, has still not recovered from the results of that fiasco, as the descendants of Isaac and Ishmael continue to assail each other in the Middle East.

Abram stumbled back to the Promised Land. Had God written him off now? Would he ever reach his potential? The answer came in Genesis 13:14–17, when the Lord gave him a message of tremendous import: "Lift up your eyes from where you are. . . ." *Don't let the experience in Egypt paralyze you, Abram; get your sights up off the ground.* ". . . And look north and south, east and west. All the land that you see I will give to you and your offspring forever. I will make your offspring like the dust of the earth, so that if anyone could count the dust, then your offspring could be counted. Go, walk through the length and breadth of the land, for I am giving it to you."

Abram is finally on his way to greatness! God's plan has been delayed, but not canceled. There will be a Hebrew nation after all.

Another spectacular example is Jonah, whose preaching brought an entire capital of the ancient world to its knees. Who would have dreamed that Jonah, the man who did his best to torpedo God's will for his life, would end up being the one smashing success among the Old Testament propehts? Taken as a group, they mostly failed. Jeremiah was consistently mocked or else ignored; Amos was thrown out of the king's court; Ezekiel was told in the very beginning that nobody would listen to him. Even Isaiah and Daniel managed only tentative responses from the monarchs they addressed.

But "the Ninevites believed God. They declared a fast, and all of them, from the greatest to the least, put on sackcloth" (Jonah 3:5). The lives of perhaps a half million people were spared as a result.

Why did the pagan Assyrians listen and respond so wholeheartedly to this man? It is tantalizing to wonder whether Jonah told them about his voyage; some have suggested that even his skin and hair might have been bleached by the acids of the fish's stomach, lending credence to his story. After all, Jesus did comment that "Jonah was a sign to the Ninevites" (Luke 11:29).

If so, the event shows us God's amazing power to turn human perversity upside down and use it for good. Even if Jonah did not relate his past on the streets of Nineveh, the results of his ministry force us to admit that mistakes can be overridden.

Had modern Christians been given the chance to counsel Jonah between chapters 2 and 3 of his book, after his return from the sea but before going to Nineveh, some of us would almost certainly have said, "Well, yes, my friend, God will forgive you for trying to run away from him, but the future is likely to be second-best from here on. You see, you've missed God's perfect will for your life, and now you must be content with whatever can be salvaged."

In so doing, we betray an overly rigid view of God's planning. We assume he has only one track for each of his children, and all other routes are sure to be bumpy detours. They may get you to heaven in the end, but you'll be exhausted if and when you arrive. You didn't stay in "the perfect will of God."

Such thinking confuses God's foreknowledge with his predestining. While he is omniscient and therefore knows all things before they happen (we will never surprise him by our actions), the Scriptures do not tell us that he has narrowed every life choice for every person down to one best option, and any other will cause the universe to wobble.

Erwin W. Lutzer reminds us in his book *Failure: The Back Door to Success* that God's perfect plan for the world got ruined a long time ago—in Eden. Thus, he concludes:

> To talk about the "ideal" life is quite futile. Since we were all born as children of wrath, we have all experienced sins and failures. The only ideal life will be in heaven, and if you are reading this, you're not there!

> Of course, within the context of our sinful human condi-

tion, God undoubtedly has a plan for everyone's life. . . . But all such plans are made by taking our sinful condition into account. For God, there are no contingencies; He knows the end from the beginning.

What if we should err on one point or another? What if we disobey God and sin greatly? Or marry the "wrong" one? God will not be caught off guard. He will not be forced to activate emergency equipment. *He is prepared to help us in our sin as He was to help Adam in his!* [1]

If God is not only the Creator but also the Creative Manager of the world, he must show at least as much creativity as human managers do. The genius of any businessman lies in how well he can shift and adjust to a constantly changing economic picture. If what has worked well in the past is starting to falter, he quickly takes note, figures out why, and revises his strategy. If one approach is blocked, he moves on to the second or third. He sees various ways to reach his goals.

Surely God is even smarter at managing people than we are.

One business seminar leader asks his audiences to imagine a railroad track going over a steep mountain. He draws a quick sketch on his chalkboard and then adds, "Now imagine that a train is starting up this side of the mountain while at the same time another train is starting up the other side. And there are no sidings along the way.

"What is needed in this situation?"

The answer, of course, is someone to intervene—someone to look down, as it were, from a spotter plane and see both trains at the same time heading for a collision. He can then take steps to prevent tragedy.

"Such a person has what I call *super-vision;* he is in a position to take in all the factors at once. That's what you men and women must do on your jobs; that's why you're called *supervisors.* You are to see what other people can't or don't see and then take action."

The Ultimate Supervisor, of course, is he who dwells in the heavens. He can see exactly what we are doing with our lives, and he has a vast array of options at his fingertips.

One day some ink was accidentally spilled onto a beautiful and expensive handkerchief. The mess was observed by an artist who decided to make the best of the situation. So he drew a picture on the cloth and used the blotch of ink as part of the scenery. God is well-equipped to do that for us, if we are prepared to let Him.[2]

The one nagging difficulty, as was mentioned earlier, comes when *other people* are not prepared to let him redeem the blotch. Some are afraid to welcome or encourage the fallen but forgiven Christian for fear of "setting a bad example." They do not want to seem soft on sin, and so they continue in aloofness. Others are downright vindictive; they are determined to serve as God's warden, not accepting the fact that the Judge has already granted pardon.

God does not force such people to change their minds, of course, and their resistance becomes a limitation on what he can do. Though he might want to restore his child to a place of service in the church, the members may steadfastly refuse to allow it. Such is indeed a tragedy.

But our God has not used up his options. Rebuffed at one point, he will simply turn to another. He cares too much to give in to the biases of individuals. The Christ who holds "the power of an indestructible life" (Heb. 7:16) will not be thwarted in the end.

The wife of a man who had lost his position due to a moral sin told of the assurance she gained from reading the small book of Haggai. The great Temple of Solomon had been burned down by the Babylonians, but now the prophet was urging the people to rebuild. Would their efforts be successful? And would God's house ever be as splendid as it once was?

"They got to work," she said, "and although some thought the new effort was poor by comparison, the Lord said in chapter 2, '"I will fill this house with glory. . . . The glory of this present house will be greater than the glory of the former house,' says the LORD Almighty. 'And in this place I will grant peace"' [vv. 7, 9].

"I'm looking forward to what God is going to do in our lives in the same way."

God's ability to redeem the past and put it to surprising use can be illustrated by the life of a tough, wiry former narcotics agent named Eddie Codelia. Born of a Chilean father and a Puerto Rican mother, he grew up in the Bronx, spent two years in technical school after high school, married his childhood sweetheart, and soon became a policeman. He was good at it; he knew what street life was about, and he was promoted to the narcotics bureau in less than a year. His part in a Harlem shoot-out, in which he killed two and wounded two others, won him New York City's Medal of Honor. "They usually give that post-humously," he notes with a wry smile.

After receiving a newspaper award for police service in 1968, he went on to the special investigation unit, which oper-ated city-wide, looking for major drug dealers. "We got into certain methods that, uh, shall I say, are frowned on by the federal government—illegal wiretapping and so forth. But we were making some big seizures and arrests, and as long as the state officials said to keep going, we did."

Next, however, Eddie and his four subordinates began keeping some of the proceeds of the arrests. Then, in 1970, headlines announced that $15 million worth of drugs was missing from the Property Clerk's office. The FBI moved in and arrested forty officers. "None of us had taken the stuff," Eddie explains. "It came out later that the Mafia had done it. But what we'd been doing got exposed along the way; fifteen of the guys turned informer and testified against the rest of us."

Eddie finally went to prison on September 28, 1976, in Al-lenwood, Pennsylvania, and found that ex-cops were especially despised in the cellblocks. He was befriended, however, by a group of men and women who came each Tuesday night to hold a Bible study. "I found out that the Christ I'd always seen on the crucifix really did exist, and that he died for *me*. At the age of thirty-four, with a wife and three kids back home wondering what would become of us all, I committed my life to God.

"Three days later, my wife made the same commitment through a church she'd started to attend. When I got paroled after sixteen months in prison, I joined her there and found a group of people who accepted us both. They didn't judge us; they helped us."

The new thing God had waiting for Eddie Codelia came in July, 1980, when he moved his family to Washington to take charge of the prisoner services department at Prison Fellowship. He is uniquely qualified for the post. "Having spent my life in law enforcement, I know how the system works, and I'm able to answer the questions of prisoners and their families who write in. They want to know about court procedures, parole board technicalities, halfway houses—and it's like I've been in school twenty years just to train for this.

"We match up the needs with service agencies and volunteers all over the nation. I can't imagine a more fulfilling job."

Neither Eddie nor anyone else would have *prescribed* that he step outside the legal boundaries, get caught, and go to jail so that he could eventually be the valuable resource person he is today. But given the factors of his downfall, God has brought about an exciting reversal of disaster. Instead of a life ruined, Eddie Codelia is a life recycled.

A number of years ago I was speaking at a church in Manitowoc, Wisconsin, a port city on Lake Michigan. My host took me that afternoon to see the harbor area. A lake freighter nearly a block long was tied up, and I stared at the gaping hole in its side that ran from bow to stern, several feet wide.

"What's happening?" I asked. "Why is there such a huge cut all along the ship?"

"They've brought her in here to overhaul her—actually to enlarge her capacity" was the reply. "They have literally sliced the thing right through the middle, jacked up the top half, and now they're welding in pieces to fill the space. When they're done, the ship will carry almost twice as much cargo as before."

I could not help thinking that sometimes human beings get ripped apart as well, and though for a time their lives are an ugly sight to behold, they become bigger people in the end. The painful surgery has enlarged their capacity to serve. God has once again shown his creative management skills, and for that we can only give him praise.

For Your Reflection

1. Can you think of any reasons why God would *not* want to restore and use us after we confess our wrong? Make a list if you can.

2. Read slowly through Psalms 30 and 103, noting all the things God does for us when we turn to him.

3. What pieces of God's new things for you are already taking shape?

---

[1]Erwin W. Lutzer, *Failure: The Back Door to Success* (Chicago: Moody, 1975), pp. 83–84.
[2]Ibid., p. 89.

Justice: We get what we deserve.
Mercy: We do not get what we deserve.
Grace: We get what we do not deserve.

Sam Wilson

The Making of a Conqueror

How? When? Where!
How will God go about bringing springtime into my life?
How long will it take?
What will happen first? Second? Third?
Will it happen here in the old situation, or somewhere else?

Once our hopes have been raised and our eyes have caught the possibilities, we are suddenly full of questions. We want to know as many details as we can; our impatience mounts as we peer into the still-hazy future for shapes of things to come.

There are no set answers, as the various profiles of individuals in this book illustrate. God's restoration plan for one person is not his plan for another. Sometimes he moves dramatically, quickly, almost catapulting the person into a place he or she could hardly have dreamed of. Sometimes God waits—seeming to do nothing—until finally he makes his move. Many times his renaissance comes in stages, gradually, a little crack of light at first, then a larger beam, until eventually we are out into full sunshine. He has his reasons, and he is hardly obliged to explain them all to us.

But we can imagine at least some of them. If we find our

135

restoration coming a piece at a time, it could be because:

- He knows *we* need a gradual reentry. We are still learning to depend upon him, and a fullblown responsibility is more than we could handle. We are still in the business of understanding grace and forgiveness, of putting names to what we have just experienced, and believing that it is really true. We have only limited energy for reaching out to help others.
- He is limited by the wariness of other people. Some are not sure whether to get close to us, for fear of "contamination." Just as we are busy sorting things out in our heads, so are they. In the meantime, our opportunities may be confined.

We must resist any tinge of bitterness toward such people; after all, they are as imperfect as we are. It is true that they shouldn't be so slow to accept us; but it is also true that we shouldn't have gotten ourselves into this pocket in the first place. We are in no position to throw stones.

We must also resist any bitterness toward God for his gradual approach. *We must not despise the early stages.* If we are only a choir member in the church now, whereas we headed up a department before; if our mistake has forced us into a different job at less pay; if family relatives are only half as warm toward us now as they were previously; if our friends invite us to be with them only occasionally—we must not give up. We must not assume we have been cursed.

Instead, we must remain steady and give thanks for the progress thus far. It is interesting to note that while 1 Thessalonians 5:18 does not say, "Give thanks *for* all circumstances," it does say, "Give thanks *in* all circumstances." We are not required to put a happy face on everything that happens or to insist that our disappointment is really exhilaration. We do not have to play games with the facts. But we can give thanks in the midst of uncertainty because of our confidence in God. He is bringing us back; he knows what he is doing; and the present is but a stage to something greater.

This gives us a touch of independence. We do not have to be so consumed with such questions as:

- How long must I "wear sackcloth" and act penitent? Am I allowed to smile in public?
- What do I do with *other people's* memories of what I've done?
- How many times must I share my inner feelings with friends, would-be counselors, et al?

These take on a different light when we keep the perspective of God as our ultimate guide and mentor. Paul once commented about a troubled Christian: "To his own master he stands or falls. And he will stand" [Note the confidence!], "for the Lord is able to make him stand" (Rom. 14:4).

We will stand much faster, of course, if the local fellowship, the church, decides to help us rather than just watch from a distance. I once asked the Rev. Randy Nabors, a Reformed Presbyterian pastor in the inner city of Chattanooga who also works with prisoners, "What gives a person hope that his life could be different in the future?"

"It takes two things," he replied. "The proclamation of the gospel—that Jesus forgives and changes, making new creatures—*linked with* the evidence of acceptance by a Christian community. The second proves that the first was more than just talk."

He went on to tell about a young man, a graduate of a Christian college in his city, who knew all the proper theology but had become a drug addict nonetheless. "He was hooked on methadone, and all the talking in the world wouldn't set him free. What finally turned him around was when one of our deacons took him into his own home for a year and a half. There he saw the doctrine fleshed out, and he was gradually restored."

Church boards and committees that read 1 Corinthians 5 (the disciplining of the man who committed incest) must go on to 2 Corinthians 2 (Paul's follow-up instruction to "forgive and comfort him, so that he will not be overwhelmed"—v. 7). The

137

Scriptures are clear in their call for spiritual leaders to "bind up the brokenhearted,"[1] to bring back the stray sheep of the flock,[2] to "restore him gently."[3] As they reach out in love, their members will do the same, and healing will result.

One man who was ousted from his profession for an indiscretion took work as a hod carrier simply to put bread on the table. He was suddenly plunged into a drastically different world; instead of going to an office each day, he was hauling loads of concrete block up to the fifth level of a construction site. Gone was the piped-in music in the corridors; now he had to endure blaring transistors. Any girl who walked by was subject to rude remarks and whistles. Profanity shot through the air, especially from the foreman, whose primary tactics were whining and intimidation: "For —— sake, you ——, can't you do anything right? I never worked with such a bunch of —— in all my life. . . ."

Near the end of the third week, the new employee felt he could take no more. *I'll work till break time this morning,* he told himself, *and then that's it. I'm going home.* He'd already been the butt of more than one joke when his lack of experience caused him to do something foolish. The stories were retold constantly thereafter. *I just can't handle any more of this.*

A while later, he decided to finish out the morning and then leave at lunchtime. Shortly before noon, the foreman came around with paychecks. As he handed the man his envelope, he made his first civil comment to him in three weeks.

"Hey, there's a woman working in the front office who knows you. Says she takes care of your kids sometimes."

"Who?"

He named the woman, who sometimes helped in the nursery of the church where the man and his family worshiped. The foreman then went on with his rounds. When the hod carrier opened his envelope, he found, along with his check, a handwritten note from the payroll clerk: "When one part of the body of Christ suffers, we all suffer with it. Just wanted you to know that I'm praying for you these days."

He stared at the note, astonished at God's timing. He

hadn't even known the woman worked for this company. Here at his lowest hour, she had given him the courage to go on, to push another wheelbarrow of mortar up that ramp. God had used a fellow believer to rescue his spirit just in time. He stayed with the job until something more suitable came along.

* * *

Whether we have the prayerful support and extended love of a church or not, we can still make it. We must not let the shortcomings of one congregation derail us. Their fears and prejudices may make it hard for us, but they do not make it impossible. Our Father will believe in us no matter what.

And we never know when he will move us from one stage to the next, or suddenly launch us out into a bold new venture all at once. "The God of all grace, who called you to his eternal glory in Christ, after you have suffered a little while, will himself restore you and make you strong, firm and steadfast" (1 Peter 5:10). We never see the full picture on any given day. Like a mountain climber struggling up a ravine, we sometimes feel isolated and surrounded by cliffs. But we must remember the goal. We are on our way to the summit. Most of the time it is not within view, but we are headed there regardless. And we will break into the clear eventually.

Along the way, we sometimes battle the fear of falling. More than one forgiven person has been tormented with the fantasy of "What if I blow it again? What if, after all this pain, I am not strong enough to resist temptation?"

The Enemy, of course, would love to engineer a repeat performance. And one of his first strategies toward that end is to get us worrying about it. The more we entertain notions of a second fall, the more vulnerable we become.

But a curious thing happens sometimes. The Devil overplays his hand just a little. If we are alert, we will realize the source of our fears. Near the end of *Perelandra*, C. S. Lewis tells how Ransom is beset in a cave once again by the Un-man, and then "something else came up out of the hole . . . branches of trees . . . then a tubular mass which reflected the red glow . . . long wiry feelers . . . the many eyes of a shell-helmeted head . . . a huge, many legged, quivering deformity, standing just behind the Un-man so that the horrible shadows of both danced in enormous and united menace on the wall of rock behind them."[4]

Notice how Ransom deals with this threat:

"They want to frighten me," said something in Ransom's brain, and at the same moment he became convinced both that the Un-man had summoned this great crawler and also that the evil thoughts which had preceded the appearance of the enemy had been poured into his own mind by the enemy's will. The knowledge that his thoughts could be thus managed from without did not awake terror but rage. Ransom found that he had risen, that he was approaching the Un-man, that he was saying things, perhaps foolish things, in English. "Do you think I'm going to stand this?" he yelled. "Get out of my brain. It isn't yours, I tell you! Get out of it." As he shouted he had picked up a big, jagged stone from beside the stream. "Ransom," croaked the Un-man, "wait! We're both trapped . . ." but Ransom was already upon it.

"In the name of the Father and of the Son and of the Holy Ghost, here goes—I mean Amen," said Ransom, and hurled the stone as hard as he could into the Un-man's face. The Un-man fell as a pencil falls, the face smashed out of all recognition. Ransom did not give it a glance but turned to face the other horror. But where had the horror gone? The creature was there, a curiously shaped creature no doubt, but all loathing had vanished clean out of his mind. . . . He saw at once that the creature intended him no harm—had indeed no intentions at all. It had been drawn thither by the Un-man, and now stood still, tentatively moving its antennae. Then, apparently not liking its surroundings, it turned laboriously round and began descending into the hole by which it had come.[5]

Such a powerful image shows us exactly what to do with fears of relapse. We must rise against them in the name of our Lord and refuse to be bullied. In the words of Galatians 5:1, "It is for freedom that Christ has set us free. Stand firm, then, and do not let yourselves be burdened again by a yoke of slavery."

God is not interested in failure. He has no reason to want to abandon us to a twilight zone of stagnation. He is committed to seeing us grow, expand, mature, and become ever more useful and fulfilled. Great numbers of his people—our brothers and sisters in Christ—share that dream as well. We can move ahead with anticipation, even excitement. We can start again.

For Your Reflection

1. Name five good things that have occurred in your life in the recent past, and then spend time thanking God for each one specifically.

2. Meditate on Scriptures that speak about *steadfastness* or *firmness,* such as:

> Daniel 6:26
> 1 Corinthians 15:58
> 2 Corinthians 1:3–7
> Colossians 2:5
> Hebrews 3:12–14
> Hebrews 6:16–20
> 1 Peter 5:6–11
> 2 Peter 3:17–18

3. Pinpoint any feelings of bitterness you may be nurturing toward persons who have been cool toward you, said unkind things, or whatever. Ask God to wash these feelings out of you and help you rise above them.

---

[1]Isaiah 61:1–3
[2]Ezekiel 34:1–16; also see Zechariah 11:15–17
[3]Galatians 6:1–2
[4]C. S. Lewis, *Perelandra* (New York: Macmillan, 1944), p. 181.
[5]Ibid., pp. 181–182.

PROFILE

The Mismatch

Charlotte Koyama arrives early at the hospital, dressed casually for the work of cleaning thirty rooms. She loads her cart with a stack of fresh sheets, checks her cleaning supplies, and moves toward her assigned corridor on the second floor.

The patients look forward to her coming, not only for the tidiness she will bring but also for the good cheer she will spread along the way. They know she is likely to pause in her dusting to look at their get-well cards, to answer their questions, to pat them warmly, sometimes even to pray with them. She will leave their spirits refreshed along with their beds.

When her shift ends at three in the afternoon, Charlotte heads to her car, arriving home about the same time as Jeff and Billy. Her older son is in high school now; her younger one has started junior high. As Charlotte prepares the evening meal, she tries to prepare her inner spirit for the arrival of her husband, Mitsuo. She cannot predict whether he will have had a good day or a bad day, but she intends to be ready.

It is not what you would call an ideal marriage. In fact, it never has been. The reasons for that have to do with how the marriage occurred in the first place and the long and difficult road it has taken since.

"I first met Mike—everyone calls him that—when I was sixteen," she recalls, thinking back to her growing-up days in Seattle. "He had come from a wealthy family in Japan and was studying at the university—he was about twenty-three. He was very bright, the kind of guy who seemed sure to succeed in life. And though he said he was a Buddhist, he didn't seem to take his religion all that seriously.

"I had become a Christian three years before, at a summer camp. It was a very real experience for me; I got involved in the church with a good group of young people, not only on Sundays but in a midweek club as well. I was eager to learn more about the Lord, since I hadn't had any spiritual training at home."

Her young faith, however, was still getting its roots when the chance came to take a two-week trip to Montana to visit relatives.

"It turned out to be a 'vacation without God,'" she says now. "I didn't do anything terribly bad, but my attitudes went through a sort of shift on that trip. I dated a non-Christian while I was there, and when I got back, it seemed like I began noticing all the faults of the people at church. The inconsistencies, the gaps between what they said and how they acted began to irritate me."

When she started dating Mike, several people expressed their disapproval. She continued to see him regardless.

"Not long after I finished high school, I began thinking seriously about our relationship. Maybe the church people were right. With a good deal of anxiety in my heart, I took the plunge. I broke up with him.

"The news spread fast, of course. The next Sunday

144

in church, a woman came up to me with a gleam in her eye to say, 'Isn't it wonderful that you've done what the Lord wants?'

"That did it! Something snapped inside of me. The church would run my life no more. Three weeks later, Mike and I were married by a justice of the peace. He was twenty-five; I was eighteen."

Her husband soon established himself in business, but the mixing of two cultures under one roof had its problems. When the young couple made a three-week visit to Japan, Charlotte understood more completely how important position and rank were in his family.

"Mike was very strict. He earned and controlled the money; I stayed home and took care of babies. We moved to a suburb of Tacoma when we could afford it, and only after a long discussion did he permit me to get a job."

She began working as a ticket agent for Northwest Orient. "It's an odd thing," she says, "but airport work changes people. The unusual hours, the mix of peak pressure times and then slow times . . . you get real close to the people you work with. Sometimes too close."

As time went on, the problems at home seemed to mount. "I had put Mike on a pedestal to replace my spiritual life. He was my new allegiance. But gradually I began to see how human he was. His god was money. And I also began to see that I had married him out of spite. I hadn't thought it through at all; I just wanted to give those church people a big surprise.

"Every once in a while I would remember a vow I had made in a meeting as a teen-ager: 'God, I will always seek to do your will.' I was afraid to just forget about that vow; occasionally I would drive back to the church where I had once attended—I'd go during the week, when no one was around, and just sit in the sanctuary there and talk to God."

But when a man at work began finding ways to be

with Charlotte, she responded warmly. Her husband spent much of his time at home sitting with his friends talking in Japanese, while she worked alone in the kitchen. Here, in contrast, was someone who wanted to get involved with her. What about it?

She summoned her courage and made an appointment to see a minister. "I really wanted to be told that it was wrong," she says. "Instead, he listened to me talk about my life for a while, found out I'd stopped attending church regularly, and finally said, 'Well, you're not living according to God's way now, so having an affair is not really that much different.'" All resistance faded at that point, and the liaison proceeded.

A number of months went by. Mike was too occupied with his growing business to even discover his wife's unfaithfulness. "But when it came right down to it," Charlotte says, "I couldn't bring myself to give my kids a stepfather. I'd had one myself—and he'd had an affair with my younger sister. So that was out, as far as I was concerned. What about leaving Mike and letting *him* have the boys? No—that was worse.

"I recall praying, 'Lord, I need help. I once walked with you, remember? Give me the strength to break off this relationship, because I can't do it alone.'"

God apparently answered that prayer when the man left his job at the airport and bought a travel agency. Meanwhile, Charlotte pondered the idea of returning to her earlier faith. Her babysitter was a Christian, as was her son's teacher at school. The teacher even talked to her at one point about Jeff's spiritual sensitivity, while she nervously studied the floor.

Two hindrances loomed before her.

1. If she came back to the Lord, what would happen to her marriage? Mike had been willing to tolerate her going to church on Christmas or Easter, but what if she started every Sunday?

146

2. Deep inside, she still did not want to be around churchy people. Her memories of past hypocrisy had not dimmed.

It was at this crossroads that some believable Christians came into her life. The mother of one of her old friends called one day to invite her to a shower. At the party, a daughter of the woman began telling Charlotte about the family's church, the vibrancy of its worship, and how she was being helped by its ministry. Charlotte agreed to try it out.

"I was hospitalized for a short time soon after that," she remembers, "and the pastor arranged to come see me. Before he arrived, I prayed, 'Oh, Lord, let this man be for real. I can't handle any more phonies. If and when I ever talk to him honestly about my life, let him be ready.'

"I was smoking two packs a day at the time, and when he came in the room, I made a point *not* to put out my cigarette. He showed no reaction. He simply asked about how I was coming along, he read some Scripture, prayed with me, and then left.

"I decided I could listen to his preaching a little more openly."

Her spiritual return went ahead slowly, taking eight months altogether. She continued to eye other Christians with suspicion, wondering whether their religion was authentic or not. She was, above all, not interested in any rules of conduct being imposed upon her. "But it seemed as if the Lord would bring various areas to my attention, first one, then another. Something I had been doing would start to cause conviction in my heart, and I would confess it. Then something else would rise in my consciousness. I had to deal with each of these, consulting with the pastor as I went along."

One Sunday she returned to the church of her teen-age years, still debating how far to go with this renewed aspect of her life. Shortly before the sermon ended, she was struck by a sentence that seemed pointed directly at her: "The Lord knows you; he knows your name, and he doesn't give up on you." The next day she went to see the woman who had first invited her to the shower. Charlotte poured out her feelings, her fears, but also her growing sense that God was definitely drawing her back to himself.

The older woman said, "Really, you can't look at people—they'll fail you. You must keep your eyes on the Lord. He still loves you; he's had his hand on you all these years." The two ended up praying together, and when Charlotte left that day, her future course was set. She was through trying to live by her own designs; from now on she belonged to Another.

At home, her recommitment to Christ did not cause immediate miracles. Her husband continued to hold his opinion that religion was a good influence on his wife so long as it didn't interfere with what he wanted to do. Sometimes, unfortunately, it did interfere. Especially when he added an off-track betting operation to the back room of his business and expected his wife to work there full-time.

"I told him I really didn't feel very good about helping people gamble on the horses at the same time I was aiding in a Sunday school class at church—I felt my example to the girls would be pretty confusing.

"He sort of frowned and then said, 'Okay—will you work for two weeks until I can get things organized? And will you be willing to entertain people in the business when I need you?' I agreed that I would."

Having failed to enlist Charlotte, he turned later to Jeff, requiring him to work on Saturdays and Sundays. The son was as reluctant as his mother. His fears were confirmed one night when an odd fire broke out in the rear of the building. The betting records were in ashes by the time the firemen arrived, so no suspicions were raised, but the losses came to more than eighteen thousand dollars in the end.

"I thought Mike would change after that," Charlotte says. "He did let Jeff quit working for a month or so, but then he made him start up again.

"The kids sometimes ask me why I don't get a divorce. We've talked about it several times, and I tell them, 'There are three reasons. First of all, it's not my place as a Christian to leave him; I can't justify it from the Word of God. Second, I doubt we could make it financially anyway. And third, maybe things will get better!' At times I really do see signs of change in Mike's attitude toward us, signs of improvement. He's even talked about getting out of gambling. Who am I to say that God can't reach him?"

Charlotte Koyama has found the strength to cope with an unenviable situation. One senses in talking with her that she in no way feels sorry for herself. She has recognized the rash decisions that brought her to this point, she has confessed her sins to God, and she is living courageously day by day, year by year, with his enablement. The new things God has for her have come in small pieces so far: the gift of a loving, supporting church; the chance to work there with groups of young people; the inner stability to keep her balance at home. She is one of those people whose restoration is gradual. She would like to have a marriage united in Christ; whether that comes to pass or not, she is determined to remain a godly wife and mother.

"I can have a one-to-one relationship with the Lord no matter what's going on externally," she explains. "The Lord is with me when I'm serving people at the hospital; he's with me when I'm worshiping and praising him at church; he's also with me when Mike walks through that door. God helps me handle whatever comes along. One of my favorite places to pray is in the middle of doing dishes. My face is turned away from whatever tension is in the air, and I just close myself in with my Father as I work."

She has seen some remarkable answers to prayer at times when her husband's lifestyle has sharply collided with hers, and the Lord has provided an exit at just the right moment. Such experiences have equipped Charlotte to counsel with other women in difficult marriages. She knows the tensions and pressures they describe, and she is living proof that while you're waiting for a breakthrough, you can go on living with poise and equanimity. "If God is who he says he is," she tells them, "he will supply our needs no matter what. God knows what he is doing, even when we don't."

A verse in her well-worn Bible is marked in red:

> How beautiful on the mountains
>   are the feet of those who bring good news,
> who proclaim peace,
>   who bring good tidings,
>   who proclaim salvation,
> who say to Zion,
>   "Your God reigns!"
>   Isaiah 52:7

"They should put those last three words on my tombstone," she concludes with a smile. "What holds me together is knowing that God reigns over my whole world. He reigns over my marriage. He reigns over my feelings, when I don't want to submit to something. He reigns over the effect all this is having on Jeff and Billy. He is the Master of it *all*—not just part—and I don't have to be afraid."

PROFILE

Joy After the Storm

When David Steiner first came as a young seminary graduate to Lake Sparrow Camp, it was not much more than a clearing in the birch and spruce forests of Ontario. The roughhewn lodge that served as both meeting place and dining hall had a leaky roof and uncaulked windows, while the swimming area needed dredging. David and his young bride, Marilee, rented a small apartment in nearby Stanton until a residence could be built on the camp property.

Seven years later, thanks to the hard work of the Steiners and a helpful synod of churches, the camp was busy, well-equipped, and financially healthy. Up to three hundred young people packed its twenty-two cabins each week of the summer, their parents came for fall and spring retreats, and their older brothers and sisters in college gathered at Christmas vacationtime. David, Marilee, and young Randy now lived in a three-bedroom chalet overlooking the lake, and David was often asked to speak to church groups about the innovative trail camping program he had launched.

151

His fall from the heights was, unfortunately, even swifter than his rise.

Among his enthusiastic staff was Jill Boudreau, an efficient, attractive woman who could teach kids to make almost anything out of leather, ceramic, or wood. She and her husband, a Stanton carpenter, had been among the first to welcome the Steiners to the little town, and when David was ready to hire a handcraft director for the camp staff, she had been a natural choice. Throughout the summers they conferred almost daily about supplies to be ordered, schedules to be adjusted, and the spiritual results they both desired among the campers.

David talks about the time when their contact began to be more than just routine.

"It wasn't a case of my having a bad marriage and therefore reaching out for someone else—not at all. That may have been true with her, but not with me. We were just together a lot, and the trouble was, I began to have feelings for her and didn't put a stop to them.

"There were times when the Holy Spirit would deal with me, even before the relationship became physical. And I would sense conviction; I would pray and ask God to help me. But there was no change in my behavior when I was around her. This happened several times, and then it seemed as if the Holy Spirit sort of stopped bothering me."

Their rendezvous were well planned, so that neither Marilee nor others at the camp suspected. The only trace was David's internal unrest. Around a roaring fire in the evenings, he was still the bright, witty camp director, telling jokes one minute but winding up his talks with questions to make the kids think. More than a few of them responded to his calls for commitment to Christ.

"On the inside, though," he remembers, "it was all I could do to cope with the day-to-day problems of running a camp. It's hard to hear the whispers of other people when you're screaming inside."

Suddenly one day, an inquiry came from an established camp outside Omaha, Nebraska, looking for a director. The thought of moving a thousand miles to an entirely new scene brought relief to his mind; perhaps he could escape the relationship that seemed to be devouring him. The arrangements were discussed with the sponsoring denomination, Marilee was willing to relocate, and as soon as the summer program ended in late August, the Steiners said good-bye to friends and Marilee's parents and headed for the United States.

"I plunged into the work of reorganizing and expanding the program," the husky, dark-haired former halfback says, "but somehow, it wasn't as easy to forget Jill as I thought. The move really didn't solve anything; it just made the phone calls more expensive. In fact, I became so desperate to see her again that I did something rather pitiful: I concocted a trip to a convention in Detroit in November just so she could drive down from Stanton and spend the night."

Her cover-up began to unravel throughout the winter, just as Marilee began to wonder why their monthly phone bill included so many calls back to Ontario. Surely her husband didn't have that many loose ends to tie. The facts finally surfaced in the spring, awkwardly. Marilee's mother came down for a visit and, having been informed by Jill's husband, broke the news to her daughter. Through her tears, Marilee cried, "I couldn't figure out what was the matter. . . . Now it all adds up."

David did not try to deny his mother-in-law's story, but neither was he ready to confess and change. "I withdrew into a lot of hardness and distance from that point on," he says. "I really turned against Marilee emotionally. To paraphrase what Jesus said, no man can love two women. It just won't work. You end up clinging to the one as you despise the other. That's exactly what happened in my case.

"My brother came to see me at one point and said, 'David, do you realize what you're doing to yourself? To your career? There are some occupations where you can get away with this kind of stuff, but yours isn't one of them. As soon as the presbytery finds out, it's all over.'

"To which I replied, 'You know what? I really don't care. I don't feel love for Marilee anymore, and I'm not going to try and fake it. Whatever happens, happens.'"

In order to escape public embarrassment, David submitted his resignation in July, citing "my inability to cope at the present time with various pressures."

The shocked presbytery urged him to take a leave of absence, to try to work out his problem and then come back. He politely declined and began looking for a job, any job, that would give him anonymity. He soon found it, selling institutional kitchen equipment, traveling to call on school districts and hospitals throughout Iowa, Nebraska, and the eastern part of South Dakota.

He would often be gone five days at a time, leaving Monday morning and not returning until Friday or even Saturday as he drove from county seat to county seat across the open plains. "That was just as well—I really didn't want to be home. As long as I could be out there by myself, making a living, I didn't have to face what I was doing to my marriage. I could stop at a phone booth to call Canada whenever I wanted, and no one needed to know.

"But when I'd come home on the weekends, it was strange—I couldn't find a lot of reasons to complain. There was never any great outburst of anger from Marilee, just sadness. She was an incredibly strong woman through it all. About all she would say is 'David, don't you want to talk about things between us? Let's talk.' I'd brush her away with 'Look—I don't want to argue with you'—and go turn on the TV or something.

154

"I did consider separation for awhile. The question in my mind was: *Does Marilee go out the window along with my career?* My principles said no, of course, and the job was providing a separation of sorts as it was. So I didn't do anything drastic; we just moved across the river to Denison, Iowa, in time to get Randy into school that September, and life went on in a kind of dull truce."

There was a tense moment one Sunday when the carpenter called person-to-person to talk to David. His message was desperate: *Please stop making contact with my wife.*

David ventured no promises. What finally did force a halt was when the new director of the Ontario camp called in the late fall. "David," he announced, "a number of people here are now aware of your illicit relationship. All I can say is that if you don't cut it off *now,* I have no choice but to expose you and her before the entire board of directors. That will, of course, result in her having to leave, and it will damage your reputation forever."

David told the man he ought to mind his own business—but when he hung up the phone, he knew he had been outmaneuvered. He would not put his lover through a public exposure. From that day on, he would make no further contact.

But would he recommit himself to Marilee? A test occurred a few weeks later when he announced a nine-day trip through the western part of his territory with his regional manager.

"Will you be back in time for my birthday?" she asked.

David looked again at his calendar. "I don't know," he replied.

Marilee brushed back a strand of her long hair, took a deep breath, and then said softly, "If you're not, I won't be here when you return."

David pondered that for half an hour, then called his manager to say, "I can't go. Can we reschedule the trip?"

*   *   *

David Steiner's intermission lasted more than three years. How much of that was needed and how much was due to his reluctance to make an open confession is hard to say. He fought throughout the first year with self-hatred and bitterness. "If you had asked me who in the Bible I was most like," he says, "I would probably have named Adam. I had gotten myself thrown out of the garden, with absolutely no chance of return, I thought. Now I was banished.

"I didn't go to church; Marilee and Randy went without me. She'd sometimes put my Bible in my suitcase when I'd get ready to leave on a trip, but I'd ignore it. I didn't read the Bible for a long time—I didn't want to be confronted. I was estranged from the Lord, too—not just her.

"The job, in some ways, was good therapy for me. For one thing, it kept me out of the house. For another, it gave me something very concrete to accomplish. There was no ambiguity; I could look back on a trip and say, 'I sold x number of dishwashers, which means x amount of commission; I drove eleven hundred miles; I made each appointment on time; I talked one state trooper out of a speeding ticket; and so on.' I didn't have to debate what to do or whether I'd succeeded or failed; I knew right away."

Sometimes while driving along, his mind would toy with a question: *What might God have to do to get my attention?* Would he touch Randy, for example? The boy seemed not to pay much attention to his parents' problems, but then again, there was a coldness about him those days—was that partly David's fault?

"Marilee told me once, a bit wistfully, that an elderly

156

woman had come up to her in church one day and said, 'You know, dear, I'm just really praying for your husband that he'll be saved.' We kind of had a nervous laugh together about that. But the truth was, the Lord was gradually pulling me back to himself. He was reminding me that I'd made a life commitment to Marilee, and that I'd only be happy as I stayed with that commitment."

The rebuilding of their relationship could be measured only in inches. "The first visible evidence of softening on my part," David remembers, "was when I found myself planning shorter road trips. After a year or so, it seemed as if I didn't want to be gone a week at a time anymore. I began figuring out how to get back to Denison on Wednesday, then go out again. My feelings were catching up with what I'd been doing out of obligation."

David eventually began attending church on Sunday mornings with his family, which put him back into contact with the Scriptures. Psalm 51 gave him the words to express his inner feelings:

> Create in me a pure heart, O God,
>   and renew a steadfast spirit within me.
> Do not cast me from your presence
>   or take your Holy Spirit from me.
> Restore to me the joy of your salvation
>   and grant me a willing spirit, to sustain me.
>   *Psalm* 51:10–12

"I came to *want* to be steadfast again, dependable, reliable. And I saw that the first thing to be restored was not my reputation or even my marriage: it was the joy of my salvation, my spiritual relationship with God. If that were right, the rest would follow."

Marilee would occasionally raise the idea of going back to a camp ministry, but David would say, "No, not yet; I'm not ready." Sometime during the second year, the pastor asked if David would be willing to help lead the boys' club on an overnight camp-out. "I sputtered and made excuses, telling him I was sure I'd be out of town that weekend. He simply said to check my calendar, and he'd call me later to see if I could. Before I knew it, I had become part of the club staff—not only to help organize games but to lead devotions, too.

"When a person is in the middle of this kind of process, you really wonder how it will come out in the end. You just have to go a step at a time. Things were gradually improving between Marilee and me; we were talking more, laughing more, enjoying each other more. We finally got to the place where we could talk calmly about the past, and I could tell her how sorry I was for what I'd done. Her forgiving attitude made me wish I'd said those things a lot sooner."

Sometimes the two would fantasize about returning to their former work. What would it be like? They assumed they would probably have to start at the bottom again in a small, run-down camp somewhere. David got up the courage to drop in at a convention of camping administrators for half a day one time, where the reception was generally cordial. One of the men who knew the full story made a point to huddle with him and urge him to think about returning.

The next fall, he took on full responsibility for the boys' club, arranging his schedule to be home for the weekly meetings. The rising happiness in Marilee's face was matched by the words of encouragement that continued to flow from relatives. David's brother loaned him a cassette of a sermon on Romans 8:1—"Therefore, there is now no condemnation for those who are in Christ Jesus." The speaker, Judson Cornwall, concluded with the story of his vision of the diary (told earlier in this book; see pages 117–120). "I listened to that tape mile after mile," David says. "It was a tremendous boost to my spirit."

* * *

With the coming of spring, two things happened in close succession to signal a new beginning. First, Marilee discovered that a baby was on the way. She and David were equally excited—"It was like a seal upon our marriage, that we really had weathered the storm and God was now giving us a new life to cherish," she says. "A girl, we hoped!"

The second thing was a phone call from the chairman of a camp board in Colorado Springs. Would David like to consider a position as director of a 270-acre facility in the Rockies?

"I absolutely panicked," David remembers. "My immediate reaction was *No way!*—only I couldn't figure out how to express that politely over the phone. He talked me into agreeing to fly out to look over the camp and discuss the position.

"I can't tell you the agonizing that went on in that blue Chevy Caprice the next two weeks as I drove to my various appointments, arguing with myself about whether I was ready. The situation was further complicated by *another* phone call from an even larger retreat ranch in Texas. As it turned out, that was entirely too high-powered for me at this stage; the Colorado responsibility would be all I could handle, if that."

The trip went well enough, the salary was acceptable, the management structure seemed friendly, and David could find no reasonable excuse to turn it down. He and Marilee continued to pray, together as well as individually, for divine guidance. When the formal offer arrived in the mail April 10, they took a big gulp and wrote back an acceptance.

Their house in Denison was sold almost without effort, and the move went smoothly. David began working in mid-May, getting acquainted with camp

159

procedures, meeting personnel, and checking over the plans that had been made for the summer. He discovered right away that two of his four activity directors were women.

"I had to do some fast thinking and praying about how I would relate to them," he says. "My first instinct was to keep my distance, to avoid any contact beyond what was absolutely essential. I've since been able to moderate that to some degree. But I suppose I'm still hesitant when it comes to developing close working relationships with women.

"I've been forced to lean on the Lord's strength, to keep remembering Paul's words about God's power being made perfect in our weakness."

An even greater challenge came his way the second week when a food salesman stopped in to see him. He made his presentation, David placed an order . . . but then the man began to unburden himself about his own personal life. He had committed adultery for the first time within the past two weeks, and he was paralyzed by two fears: What if his wife found out, and what if he had picked up a disease?

"I stood there in the empty pantry almost speechless," David remembers, "trying to listen closely to him, but thinking at the same time, *Why me?! What can I say? I was supposed to take things nice and easy for a while yet . . . why did the Lord put me in this situation?*

"I finally started to explain a few things about the Lord's ability to forgive us, and the longer I talked, the more I could sense the Holy Spirit helping me get the words out. I pulled my New Testament from my pocket and shared some Scripture with him. Tears came to his eyes; we ended up praying together."

Before the man left, David suggested that he see a doctor, to allay his fear of VD. He also gave the man his "No Condemnation" cassette tape.

"It was good for me to have to try to help someone in a situation similar to mine," David says now. "The Lord helped me through it, and in the end, I was grateful for the challenge. The guy told me later that the tape had meant a great deal."

That first summer went surprisingly well at the camp, in spite of David's late arrival to take the reins. Teen-agers from the inner city, from small towns and farms came to swim, eat, climb, compete, laugh, ride horses, and listen to the Word of God. Some of them made life-changing decisions.

And before the Christmas group arrived, a new member had joined the camp staff: six-and-one-half-pound, blue-eyed Stephanie Joy.

The next year saw the birth of a stress camping program like the one David had pioneered in Ontario. The off-season uses of the camp flourished as well.

When David Steiner thinks about past days, he does not ignore the consequences. "The truth is, I can never go back to Stanton," he admits matter-of-factly. "Satan likes to remind me of things like that occasionally, especially when I'm tired or depressed. And there are times when life gets hectic here, and I just want to jump in a car and drive across Nebraska again.

"But the Lord helps me then, too, to get my head back into the present, back to the work he's given me to do here. All things considered, I can hardly believe the Lord could be this good to us."

Marilee's comment in a letter to her sister-in-law perhaps sums it up best: "David is more like the David I married—only things are better now, because we both learned so much through our hard time."

The Restorer

If God is at all involved
with our years
on this planet . . .
if he means to do more
than just watch
from some celestial outpost—
what can we expect?
Will things go from bad to worse . . .
or from bad to better?

He is God.
And whenever he takes the reins,
whenever we give him charge,
things do not deteriorate.
They improve.
They cannot help improving.

Now to him
who is able to do
immeasurably more
than all we ask
or imagine,
according to his power that is at work
within us,
to him be glory . . .
throughout all generations
for ever and ever!
Amen.
    Ephesians 3:20–21

With Gratitude . . .

To each of the courageous people who shared their life experience with me for inclusion in this book.

To Ralph Veerman, John Sprecher, Robert Schmidgall, Charles Nestor, and others who introduced me to the above people.

To Leighton Ford, Dr. Thomas Zimmerman, Tim and Mary Senf, Dr. Richard Dobbins, John Freeman, Bob Brenneman, and many others whose insights into the process of restoration stretched my understanding.

To Bob and Marilyn Pollitt, who provided the quiet room where this manuscript was born.

To Grace, my wife, who taught me to care for those who hurt.